GOODBYE YESTERDAY

GOODBYE YESTERDAY

Gerd Treuhaft

Book Guild Publishing
Sussex, England

First published in Great Britain in 2006 by
The Book Guild Ltd
Pavilion View
19 New Road
Brighton BN1 1UF

Typesetting in Times by
Keyboard Services, Luton, Bedfordshire

Printed in Great Britain by
CPI Bath

A catalogue record for this book is available from
The British Library

ISBN 1 84624 013 1

Acknowledgments

Firstly to everyone who endured and survived the two world wars in the last century; to my wife Joan for her assistance and to my son Ralph and daughter Helen, who persuaded me to write my memoirs, I give all my love and thanks; also to Graham Payne and David Aboav for their encouragement and help in recalling the events of the 20th century as time passes quickly by.

Chapter One

'You have to sleep now,' whispered the Ward Sister.

'I can't,' I replied.

She left and returned ten minutes later with two tablets and a glass of water.

'Take these, they will help you to sleep.'

'Help me to sleep?' I replied, feeling my voice rise. 'I finished my life on March 11, 1938.'

'Shush,' said the Sister smiling sympathetically as she left the ward leaving me to sit up in bed.

To my right lay Jock, who had been there for three days after being injured in Tobruk.

To my left was William, a likeable Welshman who suffered from asthma. As a teenager he had worked in the mines and no one could understand how on earth he could have passed the army medical. He didn't want to wear the King's uniform, and since receiving his call-up papers, had spent most of his time in different hospitals. Even with his medical history, the army doctor had refused to send William into civvies again.

While enduring long days and nights with flu in a Cheltenham hospital in the second week of February 1942, the grim news that the Japanese army had invaded Singapore reached us. But that wasn't all; we also heard that the Nazis had promoted the Norwegian Quisling as Prime Minister of Norway, and that the famous Austrian author Stefan Zweig and his wife had committed suicide in Brazil.

I discovered that William felt no hatred towards the

1

Germans. On the contrary, his favourite aunt lived in the Black Forest and he had spent a long holiday there before Hitler had come to power.

William had been impressed by the cleanliness of the streets and the genuine hospitality of the Germans. Now war had broken out, he was expected to fight against these people and, possibly, sacrifice his own life. William didn't understand the Nazi movement, or their aim to conquer the world. He compared it with Mussolini's fascism. Until Italy's invasion into Abyssinia, Winston Churchill had praised Mussolini claiming that the Duce, who made 'Italian trains run on time', was an ally against communism.

'Italy was our ally at the end of the First World War, and now we are to fight against them too?' William questioned.

Opposite William's bed was Jimmy who had already survived one world war. His duties this time consisted of peeling potatoes, attending 'pay-parade' every Friday, and reporting sick as often as possible to break the monotony of army life while waiting for his 'ticket' (discharge papers).

The bed next to Jimmy was empty. Bert, who had filled it for the last four weeks, had died the previous afternoon. It was a great shock to us all and just two days before, he has been playing chess and flirting with the nurses.

I lay still, unable to sleep, staring into the open fire that crackled peacefully at the end of the ward. The flames reminded me of so many events, but these flickers were far from like the fires that symbolised the cruel days and persecution of the Third Reich. The stolen wood collected by children from debris in the mornings created a quite different heat.

I gazed at the red coal burning smaller and smaller before the flames disappeared altogether. I wondered if they too somehow 'lived'. I sometimes thought everything visible to the human eye might have some form of life, even if it wasn't how we imagined.

Pictures flashed before my eyes and thoughts ran through my mind, coming and going like ghosts. Some were of old friends and acquaintances standing around fires, pushing and shoving, trying to toast their bread in short lunch breaks. Others were of inmates wanting warmth or syrup-marmalade in exchange for cigarettes. A hundred yards away under snow-covered trees stood our political enemy of today and our fighting enemy of tomorrow. Oh, Buchenwald how can I ever forget you?

Imagining it was still 1940, I recalled Alfred, Hermann and Harry talking while searching for another station on the radio. I could see these soldiers and others with bayonets and endless girders in front of me. I was making tea for the first Alien Company. Gone were the anti-social prisoners, political prisoners, Bible students and Jews I'd been with twelve months before, toasting their bread on the fire. Now around me were children and old women begging for food and trying to keep warm.

The desperate facial expressions of those children in France reminded me of how it felt to be really hungry.

Was I still in a concentration camp? No, this was Democratic France that claimed Liberty-Equality-Fraternity on its flag the Tricolour.

Awaking early the next morning, daylight began to approach and I continued to stare at the hot coals. Unable to fall back to sleep, my mind went back again, this time to 1936 when as an eighteen-year-old reporter for the Czech newspaper *The Bohemia* I attended the opening of the Olympic Games in Berlin. Here I saw in person for the first time Adolf Hitler and when American Jesse Owens won his Gold Medal, history recalled correctly that he refused to shake hands and left the building.

A year later I was at the World Exhibition in Paris attending the International Youth Conference in La Courneuve (just outside the capital) as an observer delegate of Austria.

3

Originally, I had been invited as a member of the Austrian student section of the League of Nations, but shortly before leaving Berlin, I had been told by officials in Vienna that I should go only as an observer and not a delegate of the Austrian Youth. This was because the Austrian Chancellor, Dr Kurt Schuschnigg, had just made an agreement with Nazi Germany and did not want to offend Berlin by sending a delegate to a left-wing youth conference.

On the evening of my arrival in La Courneuve, I sat around a campfire five hundred yards from the World Exhibition Centre. I was with representatives from twenty-seven youth organisations saluting the Tricolour and singing the 'International'.

On that warm August evening and with fireworks adding to the atmosphere, we hoped that our voices could conquer the world. Here was a generation anxious to start a new world, and our voices rose with 'allons enfants de la patrie' (the voices of freedom and liberty), which, eighteen months later were to be replaced with terror and fear. Many of the delegates I met didn't make it to the end of a war they hadn't foreseen and to a time of more peaceful understanding among nations.

One of the members from the British delegation was Robert, a smart looking Oxford student. He didn't speak particularly good French and not a word of German. This surprised me, but he explained that English was the 'world language' and if someone wanted to converse with him, they should speak English.

This attitude of English visitors to the Continent was very characteristic before the Second World War. Knowing a foreign language was not essential for business with an Englishman. It was the opposite in Germany where English and French were taught at schools; especially mine in Berlin allowing me basic grasps of these languages from a very young age. Being quite good at them was very helpful to me later in life.

Robert was shocked to see Italy represented in the exhibition pavilions by a nude statue of Mussolini, which he thought was tasteless. Italy attacking Abyssinia and supporting the rebel Franco against a democratically elected Spanish government, of course, wasn't tasteless whatsoever! Now was the time that the American Ambassador Joseph Kennedy described in his book *Why England Slept*.

One thing was certain, life in Montparnasse and Montmartre in that hot August of 1937 did not reflect the political outlook of Europe. The British Pavilion wasn't very impressive, so Germany with its statue of Kolbe signifying the Nazi aims for 'Lebensraum' (living space), and Russia's theme for world revolution with its 'Hammer and Sickle' were the most eye-catching and the only obvious signs of a forthcoming international conflict.

In spite of our different opinions I liked Robert. He wasn't like the delegates from Indonesia, Sarajevo or Radavvy who went from one political meeting to another hoping the Moscow apostles would bring a peaceful future. Robert wanted to enjoy his time in Paris. He wanted to visit the World Exhibition and not take part in all the political meetings and demonstrations.

After the sun set over the Seine in the evening, the coloured neon lights gave Montmartre an atmosphere of joy and excitement. The lights lit the names of Maurice Chevalier, Josephine Baker and Lucienne Boyer in red, white and blue. After Hitler came to power in Germany you couldn't hear any Josephine Baker in a Berlin dance hall.

Jesse Owens was at least allowed to run at the Olympics, but music by black singers was forbidden under the Nazis. Only my friend Horst had one of her records, but when he was promoted in the Hitler Youth to 'Kameradschaftführer' he didn't dare listen to any foreign songs that Goebbels had banned in case he was denied further promotion. In fact he destroyed his Josephine Baker record.

5

In the first three days I attended several meetings, listened to long speeches and went to a reception given by Del Vajo, the Spanish Foreign Minister. He hoped many would join the International Brigade as the Spanish Civil War was already reaching its climax with Franco, aided by Hitler and Mussolini, odds on to win. Travellers, Communists and the unemployed were only too anxious to join the International Brigade to fight against fascism.

In reality, the Youth Congress was a farce, and coming from Berlin where the Hitler Youth song went 'Heute gehoert uns Deutschland und Morgen die ganze Welt' (Today Germany is ours and tomorrow the whole world will be ours!), I realised that we were already preparing for war.

A year before the Congress, I had prepared a memorandum containing twelve points to help abolish unemployment, and I sent it to different youth organisations around the world. It was discussed and praised by many, including the 'Young America Calling' group. I even received an invitation from the East European Congress to be one of their members, and the Bishop of Stockholm Manfred Bjoerkquist sent me a kind note.

Thus encouraged, I decided to send my ideas to Signor Ricci of the Italian Youth Organisation 'The Balilla' and also the Hitler Youth. I might have guessed the response in both cases would be negative. They simply were not interested in co-operating with other more democratic youth movements. But my memorandum did result in getting invitations to various courses and conferences including being here in Paris.

My mother, who had been to Paris before the First World War, wanted me to accept the invitation to the World Youth Conference in Paris, but warned me not to get involved in any political demonstrations or speeches. 'Don't discuss Oswald Spengler's book *Jahre der Entscheidung* (Year Of Decision) or *Untergang des Abendlandes* (Decline of Western Civilisation),' she had told me.

6

'You should enjoy Paris,' she said, adding a warning not to go with 'strange' women. As the train had slowly departed from the Berlin Zoo station, Mother had called once more, 'Please stay away from politics.'

It was easy to adhere to Mother's warning on young women because the majority I met up with were not at all politically minded and just wanted to enjoy their stay in the French capital.

On my second day, I joined up with a pretty Dutch girl named Koo for a sightseeing tour of Paris. I think Mother would be OK with this.

Her main aim was to visit every possible cosmetic and fashion shop she could find.

I took the opportunity to visit as many bookshops and newspaper kiosks as I could. This for me was a rare opportunity to freely obtain journals and papers confiscated in Berlin by the Gestapo and illegal in Germany now for four years.

In the evening we joined up with some delegates from Switzerland and went to the Folies Bergère, and afterwards to a nightclub where we had champagne paid for by the Swiss representative.

The effect of the alcohol somehow compelled me to show my step dancing skills in a solo performance on the glass floor. To my surprise it was so well received I made some extra spending money and the owner of the nightclub gave our group a second bottle of champagne on the house.

The next day some of us went to Versailles where the Western Powers signed the peace treaty in 1918 and where the German Foreign Minister Count Brockdorf-Rantzau said pointedly, 'Sie haben den Krieg gewonnen, koennen den Frieden verlieren' (They have won the war, but they can lose the peace).

However, I was now running out of spending money, so I decided to stop off at the Austrian Embassy to see if I could get a small loan.

The porter greeted me sceptically when I rang the Embassy bell, and was informed that the Ambassador, Herr Vollgruber, wasn't in town. Instead I was met by the Consul General who was intrigued by my membership of the Austrian Section of the League of Nations, and offered me 500 Francs – to be repaid to the Foreign Office on my return to Vienna. I didn't tell him I was living in Berlin where I'd only been allowed to take ten German Marks out of the country. But I was desperate for the loan and didn't say anything. I agreed to his proposal.

Twelve months later I met the Consul General under very different circumstances. We were both wearing the same uniform in Dachau concentration camp.

He remembered my visit to the Embassy in Paris and said, 'I knew that we would never get the loan back.'

Back in Paris with money in my pocket, I enjoyed my first good lunch and returned to the Exhibition, visiting the 'Buffalo Bill' Pavilion. Here I saw a visitors' book containing the signatures of famous politicians such as Sir Austen Chamberlain, Poincaré, Mussolini. Hindenburg, Stresemann, Briand and Daladier, all of whom had been pretending to work towards peace.

There was also a room decorated with flowers given by various youth organisations. Jacques Kaiser, leader of the French delegation, placed a wreath of red-white-red flowers, the colour of the Austrian flag, next to the Tricolour. But the leader of the Austrian delegation, Franz Helmut Leitner, promptly removed them saying Austria wasn't officially represented at the Congress.

To me nothing could have symbolised the European nationalism more than that small incident.

Then I attended another meeting on the Spanish Civil War, this time with the popular French author Romain Rolland appealing for volunteers.

After the meeting I wandered off into the crowd with

Dorothy, one of the members of the British Youth Delegation I had met at the beginning of the conference. We strolled through the Exhibition Centre for a while and later took the train back to the camp. It was the first time I'd been on the Metro in Paris and I was very surprised by how dirty it was. There was no comparison to the underground back in Berlin which always spotless.

We took the first train towards 'Graville' but soon realised that we should have taken the opposite train to 'Gravelotte,' so it took another hour before we reached the camp. Two years later when Dorothy visited me in Richborough, we joked about our long journey on the Metro in Paris.

The next couple of days I stayed in the camp and took the opportunity to sunbathe near my tent. One afternoon I was interrupted and introduced as representative of the Austrian Youth Delegation to three Chinese men. After bowing, one of them began to speak in Chinese while another tried to translate his speech into French. The Chinese men, who were representatives of General Chiang Kai Chek, were in Paris buying military equipment to defend their country against the Japanese invaders.

I tried to acknowledge what they said, but I could barely understand. I just nodded politely.

After the brief meeting with the Chinese representatives, I remembered a very old friend of mine, who had lodged with us in Berlin shortly after the Marco Polo incident in 1931.

At that time Japan was called the 'Prussia of the East' and my friend, a Japanese lodger Dr Gero Koizumi, was a member of the Japanese Foreign Office. He tried to teach me the Japanese language and took me to Japanese restaurants and modern exhibitions in Berlin.

He asked my mother if she would agree that he could take me to Tokyo, promising a good education at the university in Tokyo, but my mother refused his invitation. Our Japanese lodger must have been in a high-ranking position inside the Japanese Foreign Office as he was invited to tea with the Reichsprasident Hindenburg, and with the leaders of all political parties. He even had a meeting with Adolf Hitler.

After he went back to Tokyo we had several more Japanese lodgers as we lived close to their Board of Trade. It was also well known that the Japanese liked the Germans and their efficiency. When I met the Chinese Delegates, they had already been at war with Japan for seven years and I remembered my first meeting with our lodgers in Berlin.

On the final evening at the Congress, the French government invited us to a banquet on a boat moored in the River Seine. It was decorated with Chinese lanterns and after a magnificent seven-course meal, we all toasted the government thanking them for their excellent hospitality. I recalled the toast for peace around the world being drowned by the explosion of more fireworks let off from the Exhibition Hall in Paris.

It was the end of a Congress, which had chosen to completely ignore the rearmament of the Third Reich. Few of the delegates could have imagined that, just seven months later, Austria would 'disappear' and the swastika would be flying over Vienna.

Austria had already lost the sympathy of the West when Chancellor Dollfuss oppressed the Social Democratic Party in February 1934. The Nazis murdered him five months later, and the Italian Dictator Mussolini sent his troops to the Brenner Pass.

London and Paris supported his move and the independence of Austria seemed guaranteed. But it was ill founded and less than three years after that the Swastika was flying on the Eiffel Tower in Paris. On my way back to Berlin after the Congress, I stayed for three days in Cologne to meet my father. He was there trying to sell velvet cushion covers and was staying in a small boarding house.

He was very depressed because he could not enter any

10

restaurants or coffee houses which all displayed signs Juden unerwunscht! (Jews not wanted). Even in the park, Jews were not allowed to sit on the benches.

My father looked very Jewish, but he spoke perfect French, and I had a good knowledge of the French language. So we decided to go to a restaurant and pretend we were visiting Frenchmen.

It worked, and the two of us caught up with each other's news over a good meal.

To the shock of my mother and I, just two months afterwards, my father died of a heart attack in his sleep.

Back in Berlin, my mother tried extra hard to provide a meal for me. Around the city giant posters appealed to German housewives to serve an Ein-top-gericht (a one dish meal hot-pot).

All this raced through my mind as I lay in the hospital staring at the fire, which was now just ashes. Then someone snoring loudly at the other end of the ward interrupted my thoughts.

Suddenly a beam of light from a pocket torch came towards my bed. It was the Sister.

'Are you still not asleep?' she whispered. 'Would you like a cup of tea?' I nodded and she motioned me to follow her to the kitchen. Even in my dressing gown, I felt cold. It was a bitter February night. The kitchen wasn't much warmer. As I sat down at the table, Sister picked up the patients' list and, without looking at me, read aloud: 'Gerd Treuhaft, Pioneer Corps 13800430.'

She then looked at me and said, 'I see there is no name by the next-of-kin section...' And before she could ask why, I interrupted: 'I told you earlier that my life finished on March 11, 1938.'

I could see that she wanted more of an explanation, so I outlined my story:

In 1934, three weeks before the Third Reich celebrated

11

its first year in power, I received at home in Berlin my 'HEIMATSCHEIN' from Vienna. These were documents that entitled me to Austrian citizenship. At that time, being Austrian was a perfect cover to oppose the Nazi dictatorship, which was already showing signs of oppression and brutality against their opponents; although the persecution of the Jewish community wasn't very apparent yet in Berlin.

I wasted no time in getting my Austrian passport from their Embassy in the Bendlerstrasse, not far from the German Ministry of War. I realised that without my knowing, my mother must have contacted Olga Treuhaft – my real mother – to obtain the document from the Town Hall in Vienna.

I should explain. My real mother was Austrian and Jewish. She was not married and had no visible means to support me, so she took me to an orphanage in Koepenick on the outskirts of Berlin where she had been living and met my real father who was not Jewish.

My guardian, Dr Lam, who was responsible for several unwanted children, arranged for me to be fostered with Mr and Mrs Siegfried Levy – a young couple who were anxious to foster a child and who lived comfortably in a wealthy district of Berlin.

By not being adopted, I kept the name Treuhaft on my birth certificate and also the nationality of my real mother. Years later I learned that in October 1941 Olga Treuhaft was sent to the Litzmanstadt concentration camp from where she never returned. I never did get to meet her; though I did find out she went on the stage under the name Olly Treu and wrote articles for the Austrian paper *Die Presse*.

Sadly the Nazis also murdered my guardian, Dr Lam, in 1941. He was shot by the Gestapo for hiding Jewish children.

So one month after securing Austrian citizenship, the political storm in Vienna started with the revolt of the Social Democrats against the Dollfuss regime.

The Chancellor Engelbert Dollfuss was determined to

oppose a left-wing government with the help of a political group called the 'Heimwehr' led by Count Starhemberg. Starhemberg arrested the leading members of the Viennese Labour Party, including their leader Emil Maurer. They were released after a few months.

Interestingly, four years later Maurer was again arrested, this time by the Gestapo, and sent to Dachau concentration camp where I met him, being in the same hut.

Like me, he survived his incarceration and went on to play a leading role after the war in rebuilding the Trade Union movement in Austria.

With my brand new Austrian passport I made my first foreign trip and went to Leitmeritz in Czechoslovakia. I had a girlfriend, Renee from Berlin who had moved there with her parents when we were fourteen, and two of my friends had already spent a holiday in the town. But she had already found a new boyfriend, so I took the next train to Prague.

Czechoslovakia by this time had already become a refuge for many prominent Jewish journalists and opponents to the Third Reich, so I decided to contact editorial offices of newspapers printed in German and who employed German refugees.

After several unsuccessful attempts, I had better luck at a long-established German language daily *The Bohemia*. The Editor, a man named Kauder, was very friendly and, while he couldn't promise anything, was willing to consider anything I sent from Berlin.

This, then, was the first step in my journalistic career.

Back in Berlin, I soon sent off my first report to *The Bohemia*. It was about the acute shortage of raw materials in the textile industry under the Third Reich. It was printed and I was over the moon!

The paper wasn't on sale in Germany, so I had to go to the Czechoslovakian Embassy and ask the press attaché to see it.

As well as being keen on journalism and politics, I was also an avid film fan, and a couple of months after my return from Prague, the premier of a film called *Abschiedswalzen* was due to be held in the Kaiserallee, Berlin. It was the tale of Frederic Chopin with two top stars Wolfgang Liebeneiner and Saboilly Schmitz.

I just had to see it!

I knew that press and trade complimentary tickets were issued by film companies, and that very often two tickets were sent to members of the cast and newspaper critics. In February 1933 I attended my first premiere by getting a spare ticket to see the premiere of 'Morgenrot' with Rudolf Forster playing the leading role. I later found out Rudolf was a friend of Noel Coward who I interviewed thirty-five years later. It was the first premier Hitler attended as the Chancellor of the Third Reich after just coming to power January 30. I was still at grammar school hoping to get a place at university.

Luckily I found someone again with a spare ticket and was able to see the film.

Afterwards I noticed the Austrian Ambassador Herr Tauschnitz leaving the cinema as one of the guests and I decided to ask him for his autograph.

'But I am not a film star,' he said smiling.

'No Sir,' I said, 'But I am an Austrian and a journalist. I would like to interview you sometime.'

I fully expected him to refuse, but to my surprise he signed my programme and said, 'You must come and visit me soon.' Two weeks later, I called on Herr Tauschnitz and he was most welcoming. And during our meeting he introduced me to his press attaché who gave me the addresses of some important Viennese newspapers.

The Ward Sister had been listening patiently to all of this and was clearly interested in my story. She wanted to know more about my life as I grew up, so I continued.

Two weeks after Hitler came to power my mother realised I could not continue my education in the Third Reich. Looking back the only advantage I had from my real mother was the entitlement to Austrian nationality. Living in the Third Reich I was a foreigner with an Austrian passport, which enabled me to move more freely than the Jews in Germany – until the occupation of Austria.

My real father was a typical Prussian. I only met him once when my foster mother insisted on a blood test so she could claim child support. After the test proved positive, he invited us for lunch and tea at the famous Cafe House 'Josty' on the Postdamer Platz. I was nine years old and wasn't told who he was. He was referred to as my 'uncle' and I found out later he was married with two daughters.

My foster parents had a happy marriage until the economic crisis at the beginning of the 1930s. My foster father was a commercial traveller and spent weeks, even months, away from home. It eventually became apparent that he had a mistress. It's why my foster mother reverted to her maiden name Koopman. We were living on state assistance and she wouldn't have received any help with the name Helene Levy.

The Sister listened intently in the hospital kitchen but at this point in the story I asked if we should continue our conversation another day.

'No, no!' she replied. 'I would like to hear more about the true picture of Nazi Germany and how you managed to support your mother and your working career until the occupation of Austria.'

So I continued:

I was due to start my first job on April 1, 1933, but my employer, Arthur Wollsteiner, a kindly 60-year-old man who ran a small wholesale business supplying ladies' coats and jackets to retail outlets, asked me to come in two days later as the Nazis had organised a boycott of all Jewish shops.

That same day I was supposed to start work was also the

day when the Nazis seized the bank account of Albert Einstein who lived near the Bayrischer Platz and who was on a lecture tour in America. Before he left for the States, he had asked a schoolfriend and myself to help him pack all his books into several big tea chests.

My first job was really a stopgap as I had no intention of making a career in the clothing industry, but at least it got me out and about delivering items to various Berlin shops and making weekly payments to the local bank. And I was able to keep up with all the international news by visiting the local newspaper kiosks that sold foreign newspapers.

Herr Wollsteiner was well educated, speaking French and English, and had a keen interest in politics. When Hitler came to power, the wholesale and retail businesses of women dresses and coats were first to suffer because the industry was 90 per cent Jewish.

He and many of his colleagues were under the impression that the Nazi nightmare would soon be over. He, and many Jewish businessmen, thought that a strong speech by the American President, Franklin D Roosevelt against the persecution of the Jews in Germany, would have great influence. How wrong they were.

When Nazi Germany left the League of Nations, Jewish businessmen and anti-Nazis believed that London, Paris and Washington would now boycott the import of German goods and that would lead to the end of the Third Reich. Looking back it was wishful thinking.

During my daily trips to the bank, I often took the opportunity to contact the Austrian and Czechoslovakian Embassies where the press attaché gave me permission to copy reports about the Third Reich that had been confiscated from book stores by the Gestapo or banned by the Nazi regime.

I got to know of reports going into papers before the Gestapo made their rounds, so I used to warn anti-Nazi newsagents in advance so they knew what the Gestapo were looking for and could sell them discreetly.

Herr Wollsteiner had no intention of emigrating as so many Jews did at that time. He and others who decided to stay were of the opinion they should not be bullied by some painter from Austria called Hitler who wasn't even German (he obtained German nationality in 1931). Herr Wollsteiner was later sent to the gas chambers of Auschwitz.

When I completed my apprenticeship in 1936, he increased my monthly wages from nineteen to twenty nine Marks and gave me a special Christmas bonus – perhaps for supplying him with illegal newspaper cuttings and information giving hope that the end of the Third Reich was in sight.

This welcome increase in my salary together with rent from two rooms at our three-room apartment meant that mother and I could keep a roof over our heads. I also took an extra job selling newspapers and my mother began selling handmade pillows and handkerchiefs to help pay our way.

Then on March 11, 1938 Hitler occupied Austria and I realised I should think about emigrating. Mother was shocked when I told her and didn't want to be left on her own. We had been through so much together.

Two weeks after the occupation, the Leipziger Strasse in Berlin was crowded in spite of heavy rain. At about 4.30 p.m. I was sent to the post office to get some stamps.

On my return to work, Albert the liftboy looked anxious and told me there were three men waiting for me on the third floor.

Albert and I were on very good terms. He had once been a member of the Communist Party's youth organisation, which was disbanded when Hitler came to power. In order to secure his job Albert joined the Nazi Trade Union. I realised that now he had a real opportunity to impress his new masters by not warning me about my visitors, but his conscience got the better of him.

17

We both knew it was the Gestapo who were waiting for me upstairs.

All I had on me was two or three Marks and the postage stamps. What could I do? Albert generously offered me what little money he had, and I thought about the possibility of catching a taxi to the Czech Embassy to see Dr Camille Hoffman, or head for Professor Henri Jourdan of the French Institute. Both men were fervent anti-Nazis.

Dr Hoffman might have helped me, but he would have had to consider his diplomatic status. Also he had already disappointed me once by stopping me at first from sending my articles to *The Bohemia* in Prague through the press attaché's diplomatic bag (a suggestion made by the paper's Editor, Dr Kauder). The Gestapo never censored these. 'I can give you good advice,' Dr Hoffman told me, 'Keep your hands off journalism.' This meant that I had to take the risk of sending my articles by normal post.

However, once Dr Hoffman saw my articles being published in Prague he told me I could come to the Embassy to see them. Eventually he said, 'I think you are going to become a good journalist,' and was prepared to accept my contributions and send them via the diplomatic bag. These included my observations about the Hitler Youth, which were of great interest to the paper. I had become a very welcome guest at the Czech Embassy and was recognised as the Berlin correspondent for the paper.

I met Henri Jourdan at a reception given by the French Institute in Berlin for a student exchange programme between Germany and France. The French Ambassador François Poncet was supposed to be there, and I thought it would be interesting to interview the Ambassador about an exchange of Austrian and French students.

Werner von Siemens Realschule, chairman of the German Football Association, was there, and so was my former French teacher Mr Martin, and Latin teacher Professor Dux (the

18

Professor's sister was the famous opera singer Claire Dux who had an affair with German film star Hans Albers before emigrating to the USA to marry the man who invented corned beef!)

At the last minute the French Ambassador had to cancel and the Director of the Institute Professor Henri Jourdan took his place.

The evening turned out to be a great success and the Professor invited me to a concert given by Maurice Maréchale. Before meeting him again I visited the Culture attaché of the Austrian Embassy Prince Schwarzenberg. I told him about my idea of an exchange between Austrian and French students, but the Prince – who wanted to be addressed as 'Your Highness' – wasn't interested and I had the impression he had already accepted Hitler's aim for a greater Germany including Austria.

I remembered that when I'd last spoken to the Professor he warned me to leave Berlin as soon as possible.

But I did not know whether the Gestapo had already been to my home, and anyway, they would be carefully watching both the Embassy and the Institute.

I thanked Albert for his kindness but decided to face the men on the third floor. As soon as I entered the office, the Gestapo men showed me their credentials and asked me to accompany them.

Herr Wollsteiner and the others were speechless, and even Albert, who was always very talkative, was silent as he watched me step into the waiting Mercedes with my two escorts.

I imagined they would take me to the local police station, but instead we ended up at my home at No. 9 Rosenheimerstrasse.

Chapter Two

The two Gestapo men didn't talk very much. My mother was standing in the corridor, and as soon as she saw them she realised what had happened.

'We want to take your son to the police station for interrogation,' said the taller of the men to my mother, 'But we would like to see his books and his correspondence first.'

Then he asked me where I kept them.

Immediately after the occupation of Austria I had destroyed everything that had an anti-Nazi leaning. Only non-political published articles were still in my archives, and some letters of support from the various youth conferences I had attended.

One of the Gestapo men looked at the letters. First there was one from Nobel Prize winning author of 'Gösta Berlings Saga,' Selma Lagerlof. Then he saw the one from the Bishop of Stockholm, Dr Manfred Bjorkquist, who had been in touch with me. Finally there was my note from Mussolini's personal secretary, but he just smiled at me and said, 'These letters won't help you any more.'

My mother was told the interrogation might take some time, and she shouldn't expect me home for supper. So she prepared some egg sandwiches for me while trying hard to convince the Gestapo men that I was innocent.

'He is only 19 and has never belonged to any political party,' she pleaded. 'How can he be guilty of any crime?'

I tried to think what might have led to my arrest, and then it came to me. Two days earlier I had enquired at the local police station whether my Austrian passport was still valid.

On reflection, it was a stupid thing to have done.

On the way to the waiting car outside, I could see my mother watching from behind a curtain, crying her eyes out. Maybe she was thinking that if she hadn't stopped me from leaving Berlin immediately after the occupation of Austria, I would never have been arrested.

As we sped along in the car, one of the Gestapo men said to his colleague, 'I don't think his mother knew about the political activities of her son.'

Suddenly we screeched to a halt. It wasn't at the police station but beside the Luetzow Canal in Berlin, where the bodies of Communist leader Karl Liebknecht and Rosa Luxembourg were found.

'If you jump, you can save yourself and us a lot of trouble,' smirked the driver. I ignored the remark, and we drove on with the two of them laughing.

I was still convinced that the Gestapo had no right to arrest me because I had not written any articles since the occupation of Austria. All my contributions had been published when Austria was an independent state, and I had complied with the law. But I was soon to find out that legal rights meant nothing to this new dictatorship.

At the police station I had to empty my pockets and take out my shoelaces in case I tried to commit suicide. I didn't understand the logic of that as, only minutes before, the Gestapo men had suggested I jump into the canal!

After several hours in a cell, I was led to my first interrogation and was again asked about my journalistic activities. Then my fingerprints were taken and I was hustled into a cell were there were other prisoners.

'Now they are arresting children,' muttered one as I was pushed inside. 'Have you anything to smoke?' another asked. I said I didn't smoke, but that I did have some egg sandwiches.

'Keep them, you will be glad of them later,' he replied. But I insisted, and we all shared Mother's sandwiches.

'How do they celebrate Austria's annexation by the Third Reich?' asked the oldest cell-mate, who was a former Communist counsellor, and already had four years' concentration camp behind him.

Another cell-mate was a former member of the Nazi stormtroopers. He was waiting for a court hearing because, when drunk, he had remarked, 'Hitler is okay, but that club-foot Goebbels talks too bloody much!'

One of my other cell companions was accused of belonging to a group that had prepared an attempt on Hitler's life when he entered Vienna. 'They are mad. I didn't know anybody who wanted to kill Hitler.'

Two days later, I was again taken for interrogation. 'Don't refuse to sign a protocol if they ask you to,' advised a cell-mate who knew Gestapo methods. 'They will force you, and you can save yourself a lot of trouble. If you are lucky, they may even give you a cup of coffee and offer you a cigarette. It depends on what mood your interrogator is in.'

I was lucky in that I was simply asked if the student section of the League of Nations was a political organisation and how long I had been a member. I told him it was not politically motivated and I was allowed to go without any physical violence.

Two weeks after my arrest, my mother paid her first visit. We sat opposite each other in a special visiting room, guarded by a policeman who made sure no personal contact took place. For a moment, we didn't know what to say, then my mother said, 'Gerd, don't lose your nerve. I will do everything I can to get you out of here.'

I just nodded and asked her if she had seen 'Uncle Heinrich', she knew I was referring to Professor Henri Jourdan, director of the French Institute.

'I have visited all your friends,' she replied softly.

I thought Henri or my friend from the Czech Embassy could still help me, but my Communist cell-mate told me he didn't think they could help as I wasn't French or Czechoslovakian.

'How can they intervene?' he added.

He was right, and a week later I received a red document from the Gestapo saying I was to be taken into protective custody having offended the German state and its Hitler Youth. There was a document to sign and it felt as if I were signing my own death warrant. I knew then that I would eventually end up in a concentration camp.

A few days later, having heard about my transfer, my mother visited me again and said she had contacted a lawyer hoping to prevent my departure.

When she had left, I was taken to a different cell where all the prisoners had either completed their sentences or were waiting to go to a 're-education camp,' better known as a concentration camp.

There was one wealthy man, Herr Bauer, who was entitled to special food, all the morning papers and a daily supply of cigarettes. He had just finished his sentence for tax evasion.

Another prisoner was accused of possessing pornographic literature and a book entitled *Hitler In Caricature*. There was also a 17-year-old boy in the cell who had distributed an illegal Communist newspaper but had never been an active party member.

Then there was a former officer of the German Reichswehr, who was arrested for subversion inside the army. He was a member of a right-wing organisation that supported the return of the Germany monarchy.

One evening, the cell door opened after the lights-out had sounded, and a young drunkard was pushed inside. For the next three days he was sent for interrogation but always refused to tell us what had happened.

By this time the rest of us realised he was a homosexual, and the Gestapo were anxious to find his friends. Eventually they gave him money so he could meet them in the café houses, and as soon as he did so, his friends were arrested.

After his revelation, we were all very careful about what we said to each other; there was always the chance that he might now be spying for the Gestapo. We were relieved when he was finally sent to face court proceedings.

Our days in prison were very monotonous. We more or less lived on rumours about a forthcoming amnesty. The first was in January, on the day Hitler came to power; then there was speculation that we might be freed on Hitler's birthday; then it was Easter, or the first day of May, followed by the annual party rally in Nürnberg, or the day of the harvest festival or even Christmas.

We might have guessed there was to be no amnesty; it was simply a ruse created by the Gestapo to avoid an increase in prison suicides.

Before the Holocaust, the Nazis had a special policy concerning prisoners. They were anxious to make deals with the Pope regarding Catholic inmates, while the Jews were going to become an object of trading with Jewish financial circles in New York, London and Paris.

Even the Communist prisoners had a special role to play when the German-Russian negotiations started.

All too often, the treatment of the prisoners in the concentration camps reflected the foreign policy of the Third Reich. The non-aggression pact between Nazi Germany and Soviet Russia in August 1939 led to the release of thousands of political prisoners from various camps.

I knew then that it was only a question of time before I was sent to a concentration camp, and I was hoping that my mother would succeed in getting emigration papers in time for me.

One cell-mate suggested that when the prison doctor next came, I should pretend I had an appendix pain. This, he said, could delay my departure for another two to three weeks and give my mother more time to secure my release.

When the doctor made his visit, I chewed a cigarette that not only gave me a temperature but also made me look and feel sickly. But on that particular occasion, another twenty or so other prisoners had all reported sick, and the doctor decided to see us in alphabetical order.

By the time my initial T was called, the effects of sickness had long worn off and the doctor reported only minor digestive troubles. It did not prevent him signing me fit for the concentration camp.

Before leaving the prison cell, I was involved in another incident that almost led me to the gallows. Every other day we were led into the courtyard for a twenty-minute exercise, supervised by the police.

It was strictly forbidden to talk to each other, but the man standing next to me suddenly whispered that he had seen me before, but couldn't remember when or where. I didn't know him, but he insisted, adding that he was being charged with high treason against the Third Reich.

Two weeks later, I found myself standing next to him during our exercise. He looked depressed. 'This will be my last walk,' he whispered. 'I am facing the guillotine. Someone has given the game away.'

I dared not speak to him again after that for fear that I could be accused of conspiracy. After all, he had said that he thought he knew me.

On my next walk in the courtyard, he was no longer among us.

On May 30, 1938, I was ushered into a large hall in the cellar of the police station. It was packed with prisoners of all nationalities either being transferred to a camp or being expelled from Germany. There were thieves, embezzlers, sex offenders and spies. They were chattering away in Polish, French, Italian and even Russian. No one knew what was going to happen to them as they were from countries with which Nazi Germany still had diplomatic relations.

I still foolishly hoped that my mother, with the help of Uncle Heinrich or the Czech press attaché, Camill Hoffmann, would have been able to obtain papers for me to be expelled to either France or Czechoslovakia.

But I knew this was not to be when I found myself handcuffed and pushed with several other prisoners into a police wagon. It was now three o'clock in the morning. I could hardly move and had especially rough treatment (even though in some German counties there were strict rules that prisoners under the age of 21 were not allowed to share a prison van with another prisoner!)

Shortly before leaving the station, a kindly policeman whispered to me, 'Keep your spirit. The time will come when you will be free again.'

I remembered those encouraging words throughout my prison life.

The next stop was the notorious Brandenburg prison, the largest in Prussia, where after 12 hours, I was moved to a prison cell in Halle.

Here two more Jewish prisoners, a fur dealer and a butcher joined me. The butcher had already spent four years in prison for sleeping with a non-Jewish girl, and the fur dealer was accused of having cheated his customers.

Both had been told they were going to a re-education camp, and, for the first time, the name of Dachau was mentioned.

After staying 24 hours in Halle, our next stop was Leipzig, where the headquarters of the supreme high court of Germany was situated.

'You are in good company here,' said the warden as he opened my cell door. He was right. The former Austrian Chancellor, Dr Kurt Schuschnigg was on the same floor. On the second floor was Pastor Niemoller, who was on a transfer to be 're-educated'.

From Leipzig we made our way to Nuremberg where the

Nazis held their annual party rallies. The police there not only handcuffed us but cuffed our legs as well. This was extremely painful as we had to march through the city in step with our guards.

The journey continued and we found ourselves in Munich where two more prisoners joined us, one of whom had already served 15 years for murder.

While seated next to me he gave me some advice, 'First, empty all your pockets so no one can find a name or address which could be fatal. And talk as little as possible. Do not contradict the SS men and do not trust any of your cell-mates.'

He reminded me of the old German proverb, Reden ist Silber, Schweigen ist Gold (Talking is Silver, Silence is Gold). This not only applied to my prison life, but later, too, in the army.

The last call of this seemingly endless journey was the Prinz Albrecht Palace in Munich, where the Nazi movement began and which had one of the biggest prison halls.

After being unloaded from the lorries, and marched through the streets in handcuffs we arrived in a huge cell. Every 10 minutes, the doors would be swung open and more prisoners would arrive for interrogation, or be transferred to a camp.

One of the prisoners, Schwarz, had just come from Dachau. He was a staunch anti-Semite.

'If you are a Jew and you are being sent to Dachau, you might as well commit suicide now,' he kept saying.

To my great surprise, six months later in Buchenwald I met up with Schwarz again wearing the Star of David on his prison uniform!

Two days after arriving in the Prinz Albrecht Palace, new guards arrived. This time they were not members of the Bavarian police, but the SS.

It was June 11, 1938 and a very hot summer's day when we arrived at Dachau.

First our clothes were taken away and we were pushed under a cold shower before being given a camp uniform.

Then we were marched to the camp barber for a close-cropped haircut then, at the double, to the gate of the commander's office.

Here we were 'greeted' by 'Oberkommandant' Roedel, SS Sturmbannführer Gruenewald and SS 'Scharführer' Lutje-Meyer with punches and kicks and told to sit knees-bent with our arms stretched out from 11 o'clock until 6 o'clock. Much of this time was in blazing sunshine.

Every time an SS guard passed we received a prod from his bayonet and, immediately afterwards, were forced to resume our position.

That was our welcoming reception at the notorious concentration camp of Dachau.

Chapter Three

A lovely summer's day came slowly to an end when the working parties returned from their work places outside the camp. We newcomers were still standing outside the Commandant's office.

Commandant Gruenewald and the so-called 'Devil of Dachau,' Luetje-Meyer shouted they would like to inspect the 'new birds,' as they called us.

I was standing at the end of the queue. Luetje-Meyer, who was reading out the Gestapo documentation of each prisoner to the Commandant, finally stood in front of me.

'You can prepare yourself for ten years here in Dachau – if you survive,' he smirked, slapping me hard twice around the face.

I remember the number they gave me – 15642. Some numbers you never forget.

At that time, I was determined to survive. Even after ten years behind the electrified barbed wire, I would still be only thirty.

After this 'reception' we were led to our hut 15/2 where the foreman gave us something to eat and showed us our sleeping accommodation – straw mattresses on the floor.

I was too tired to talk to anyone and quickly fell asleep.

The sirens rudely awoke us at 4.30 a.m. and the foreman ordered me to clean the hut, collect lunch boxes and then, with another prisoner, collect the coffee bucket.

Then came the first roll-call. Along with the other newcomers

I was assigned to a special working party where a well-known sadist named Sterzer was in charge. Because there were so many of us coming to the camps, the elder political or criminal prisoners who had nothing to do with opposing Nazism – but were still in prison on other offences – were ordered to help take charge of those imprisoned for opposing the new regime or later just for being Jewish.

Sterzer, who had murdered his three-year-old daughter, had already spent many years behind bars before coming to Dachau.

His working party, I soon learned, were known as the 'suicide commandos' and I was told I'd be lucky to survive two weeks under his brutality.

Marching to the gravel pit, I noticed two brothers next to me whose faces were very familiar, but I didn't dare ask them their names as talking was strictly forbidden.

Whenever Sterzer shouted at them, he called them 'Aristocratic swines!' For some reason Sterzer enjoyed picking on me, even kicking and punching me from time to time. The brothers would sometimes look over and I think they felt sorry for me.

I found out later that the brothers were Max and Ernst von Hohenburg, sons of the Archduke Franz Ferdinand, whose murder at Sarajevo started World War One.

The Austrian prisoners addressed each of the brothers as 'Your Highness,' but the German prisoners called them simply Max and Ernst.

The brothers were fortunate because after just four days under Sterzer they were transferred to the plantation far outside the camp under a foreman who was known for his good treatment of fellow prisoners. They survived their days at Dachau and lived quietly in Austria after the war.

Just how they managed it was never really known, but it could have been bribery. Each prisoner was allowed a small amount of money each week from relatives and friends, and they could either open an account with the camp administration or transfer some money to fellow prisoners.

My mother couldn't afford to send me much money each week, so I could hardly buy myself an easy job. Which is why I became the longest 'survivor' in the gravel pit under Sterzer. (I later found out she had written to my real father asking for assistance, but he declined declaring I had 'insulted the Führer'.)

I also worked three afternoons under a new foreman, a political prisoner who only had one arm and never shouted at his fellow prisoners. He was a former member of the German Reichstag, and after World War Two became the first leader of the Social Democratic Party in Bundestag. He was none other than Dr Kurt Schumacher.

The hut where I lay on a straw mattress at night had just been completed and was also home to other personalities during those darkest of days. My fellow prisoners included film stars, politicians, journalists and businessmen – all of whom the Gestapo had arrested after Hitler invaded Austria.

There was Paul Morgan, a film star who was a friend of Max Hansen, the man who discovered the Swedish actress Zarah Leander – and Fritz Gruenbaum, a much-liked compère in Berlin and Vienna, told me he had known my real mother.

There was also Austrian Trade Union leader Emil Maurer, who had already been arrested under the Dollfuss regime, and had been arrested a second time. Herr Kolischer, publisher of the 'Vienna Kurier' joined us in Room 2 on the block with Kurt Fuss, Hermann Leopoldi and Baron Popper, the brother-in-law of the famous opera singer Maria Jeritza. Also Herr Mahler, director of the well-known 'Remsma' cigarette factory, was another famous personality with whom I shared my confinement.

Another of my room-mates was Maximilian Reich a one-time editor of a leading Austrian paper who had given Hollywood producer Billy Wilder his first newspaper assignment.

Austrian prisoners always blamed the Germans for their fate, but they ignored the fact that the people of Vienna had given Hitler a much greater ovation than the Germans did on January 30, 1933.

Nazism was not a typical German ideology, but was imported from Austria.

Behind the electric barbed wire, there was no real unity among the prisoners. Only myself and another called Victor Gronfein were on good terms with our Austrian fellow inmates.

Victor, who had been in prison for his anti-Nazi activities, had run a bookshop in Berlin. For many months he had managed to sell 'illegal' books imported from other countries right under the noses of the Nazis.

'I used to put them in the window but with covers from famous Nazi books, such as *Mein Kampf*,' he enjoyed telling me.

It wasn't until one customer, who turned out to be a member of the Gestapo, insisted that he be given the so-called *Mein Kampf* in the window and not one from under the counter that Victor's game was up.

In September 1938, shortly before the Munich meetings that tried to avoid the start of the war, I was transferred from Block 6, room 4 to Block 4, room 3 and assigned to another working party. Here in charge was the son of the former Prime Minister of Bavaria, Egon Eisner. Being his son was his only 'crime'.

However with war becoming inevitable, Dachau prepared to become a prisoner of war camp, and after a four-month stay we were moved to Buchenwald.

The journey started with one hundred and fifty prisoners being herded like animals into railway wagons, each guarded by two SS men.

We had to lie on the floor with our hands behind our heads, staring at the lights in the carriage ceiling. And you dared not move.

Once, when the train suddenly stopped for no reason, one man leapt up and jumped through the window. There was a single shot, and he was hauled back into the carriage, and thrown bleeding to death next to his brother. There was nothing we could do to help him.

In Buchenwald, we were given new numbers so now I became prisoner 8880. The wooden barracks could not compare with the 'luxury' ones at Dachau. My new inmates included the former member of the SPD and German Reichstag Karl Bartl, and the leader of the Austrian Monarchist Party Baron Wiesner. I was still one of the youngest in the camp.

One of the more curious prisoners already at Buchenwald looked different to everyone else because he was the only one without his head shaved. He wore the same prison clothes but wore a red triangle (for political prisoner) on his tunic.

'Who is he?' I whispered to my neighbour.

'Him? He's No. 200,' came the reply and we had to shut up because an SS guard had suddenly appeared in the doorway.

No. 200? I was curious to find out more about this prisoner who was allowed to roam the camp as if he was the Commandant himself.

At roll-call I learned that his name was, apparently, Tony. Later, I was able to find out that his full name was Tony Lener. But who was this Tony Lener? Maybe he was a Nazi spy, but if he were, then letting him wander about like that would have been too obvious.

One day, when I was working on my own, hacking away at a tree with an axe, No. 200 stood beside me.

'How are you getting on?' he asked.

I could just about understand his Bavarian dialect. 'Let me show you the best way to use the axe,' he said, taking it from me.

I couldn't resist asking him about his hair. 'Why haven't they shaved you like the rest of us?'

He smiled, and replied, 'I am what you might call an honorary prisoner. I once saved Hitler's life.'

I could hardly believe what he was saying.

'You saved Hitler's life?' I gasped incredulously. 'Why did you do that? How did it happen?'

'I was a Nazi follower for a long time,' he began telling me. 'I actually still believe that Nazism is good for the German people. I was one of the first members of the party and attended every meeting before it was even known of outside Bavaria.

'Then we prepared for the famous revolt of November 9, 1923. I was marching with Hitler, Strasser and Goering to the Feldhernhalle when the Führer stopped. News had reached us that the government troops were assembling in a neighbouring street. We marched another 200 yards then suddenly I saw in the distance a man aiming a revolver at Hitler.

'For once my slow moving Bavarian brain worked like lightning and I took three strides forward and one sideways before falling to the ground with a stinging pain. I had a bullet in my abdomen, but Hitler had been saved.' (Hitler writes in his own biography from 1934 that he saved another man's life in a shooting that day!)

Hitler was very grateful, of course, and paid visits to No. 200's Bavarian estate. The trouble was, No. 200 enjoyed a drink and during one Hitler visit, drank a little too much and talked much too much.

He probably said things he shouldn't have which upset Hitler.

'Anyway, the Führer put me under house arrest, but we were still very good friends,' No. 200 told me. 'However, one evening I got really drunk. I was fed up with everything and told friends just what I thought of the Third Reich and how I felt they had deserted the party line to become capitalists.

'I had no intention of harming the state, but when Hitler

36

got to hear of it, I was arrested and sent here as an "honorary prisoner". I was greeted by the second in command who said, 'Well the guest of the Führer has come to be reformed,' but as a former high-ranking SS leader, I was allowed to keep my hair. Otherwise I am under the same restrictions as the other prisoners.

Soon after that he was removed to another camp and that was the last I saw of him, though after the war when American troops entered Bavaria, No. 200 was found alive in a small prison camp. The man who could have avoided the creation of a Third Reich and with it the outbreak of World War Two had managed to live to tell the tale.

Here in October 1938, No. 200 was just one of now nearly 10,000 of us standing and marching as prisoners every day at 5.30 a.m. on the large parade ground for roll-call. Such regular routine turned us into robots and we all thought: 'How much longer will we be able to endure this torture?' You still dared not speak. If an SS guard saw your lips move you were in trouble. The punishment for this 'crime' could be either being hung on a tree for an hour or 25 lashes with an iron whip. The latter could cripple you for life even if the gates to freedom were ever opened again.

In November, six weeks after my arrival at Buchenwald, came the notorious Kristallnacht. At the German Embassy in Paris, a young Jew, Herschel Gruenspan, shot Ernst von Rath and the Holocaust was unleashed. With the shooting being used as an excuse to arrest Jews, we began to see lorry loads of civilians then turn up at the camp.

In a special fenced off small camp, 5 so-called 'emergency huts' were put up and all the new Jewish prisoners were forced inside. In some cases more than 2,500 prisoners were packed into a single hut where it was standing room only.

Their heads were shaved as if they were dangerous criminals, with boys as young as 14 and men over 80 forced to endure hours of standing to attention.

Driven half insane and unable to bear the hellish conditions any longer, some ran madly against the electrically charged fence at roll-calls. Heading for certain death, the guards on the machine-gun tower still opened fire.

Others broke the panes of windows and cut their arteries. Some fell into the open-dug latrines in the darkness and suffocated in misery.

On the first night, SS men went into the huts, picked out Jews at random and took them outside to be flogged with steel birches, or killed with clubs. Throughout the night I heard shots and cries of mortal terror.

My hut was close to the emergency huts and in the morning I was ordered to take buckets of food to our 'comrades of race' and help fetch in the dead.

Over the following weeks more lorries arrived from all parts of Western Germany and Austria, and as the unfortunate occupants were hurried out, the guards tripped them, kicked and punched them and hit them with rifle butts.

Then, as soon as the SS guards had finished with their new victims, the criminal prisoners took them to another special compound that had been erected.

It was here that wallets, watches, rings, and even wedding bands were taken. The old men who had gold crowns in their teeth were knocked unconscious and pushed into an open lavatory where they suffocated. Everything disappeared, although at first we had no idea whether the criminal prisoners kept their spoils or handed them over to the SS. We could only suspect they were involved because the SS guards didn't have permission to take anything and could only keep an eye on these barbarians from their watchtowers.

Similar to at Dachau, there was a special category of criminal prisoners here at Buchenwald who took on authority over the Jewish inmates. They had either served long prison sentences for murder, manslaughter or theft in German jails, or were considered criminal for being Communists. Their sentences ranged from ten to twenty years, and Buchenwald was where many came to be 'reformed' into good citizens of the Third Reich. Such prisoners were put in charge of the inner camp administration.

Among them was 'Lageralteste' (head prisoner) Richter, who acted as the close adviser of the SS Commandant. His criminal pals all had key jobs and were Kapos (Captains) in charge of the working parties.

This gave the criminal prisoners great power over the lives of thousands of their fellow inmates. The so-called re-education for these gangsters was one of the most sinister moves of the Nazi concentration camp policy.

With the number of Jewish prisoners steadily increasing, it was only through the creation of hate and mistrust among the criminal prisoners that the SS was able to control them all with just two companies.

The criminals had certainly formed a very powerful organisation inside the camp and during this period they were the complete masters.

Even on pay-day a criminal would stand alongside the SS paymaster to confirm our name, prison number and what we received. Later they came to us for their commission.

At the SS canteen, they were the only ones in the camp allowed to buy anything like biscuits, chocolates or cigarettes – so if we wanted any goods we had to hand over our money to them first. Out of our 15 marks, we were lucky if we received goods worth 5 marks; the rest went into the pockets of the criminals who, in turn, used some of it to bribe the guards.

During the second week of December I was attached to a new working party. It wasn't the same as the previous ones where we had built roads, huts or uprooted trees. This one was completely different.

With a fellow prisoner I was told to report to a so-called 'First Aid' hut where we heard moaning and saw the heads

39

of Jews clotted with blood from their beatings. Some were dead and just left on the floor, or almost dead and couldn't even get a glass of water, let alone any medicine.

Our orders were to pick up the dead bodies and carry them to a small hut that had been built a few hundred yards from the electric fence outside the camp. Here we had to wash the corpses with a kind of disinfected water, put them in a coffin, and write the name and number of the dead prisoner on each side with chalk ready for cremation. A lorry would then come to collect the coffins and deliver empty ones.

This was after we had stacked them in alphabetical order. Germans love being methodical and for the Nazis, there was no difference between counting sacks of potatoes or coffins loaded with corpses.

For the first few days I found this 'work' very difficult, but my fellow prisoner had more experience and said 'You'll get used to it.' He tried to lighten the mood by saying jokingly 'I wonder what our bodies will look like before going to Weimar?' I didn't find his remark funny, but when the bitter cold wind whistled around my ears and nose, and the tips of my fingers seemed to have lost all their feeling, there were times I wished someone else was doing my job and I was the corpse.

I kept telling myself that having seen so much awful misery, I could not be afraid of anything more. To keep sane, I told myself that the bodies I was heaving into the coffins were now liberated; they were free and could not be tortured any more.

Whenever the lorry from Weimar arrived, the SS guards watched us closely and regularly opened a coffin at random to make sure than no one was trying to escape by hiding inside. Otherwise they left us in peace. The guards knew we were taking men to their graves, and they had some respect for the fact these bodies were making their final journey and were no longer an enemy to the Third Reich.

40

I began thinking that only a miracle could save me now. The big notice we saw when arriving for the first time at the camp entrance, Arbeit Macht Frei (Work Brings Freedom), really didn't mean a thing. None of the thousands of prisoners who trudged through those gates ever believed that only his work would gain him his freedom. The aim was simply to survive each day as it came.

The winter of 1938 started late in Ettersberg, site of the Buchenwald camp and home to Johann Wolfgang von Goethe. Johann wrote *Faust*, Germany's greatest literary work and a masterpiece of the 19th century that had been translated into all European languages and taught in German schools. Herr Goethe could never have imagined that where he walked for peace and concentration from his little house in Weimar could later become a place of such horror and brutality. He would have turned in his grave if he knew what had gone on here between 1937 and 1945.

Nobody in the dark forests here even referred to *Faust*. Thousands of prisoners didn't even know that Buchenwald was once a pilgrimage centre of German poets.

The Third Reich had long ago transformed this famous place into an infamous hell. It had become a place where humans destroyed their countrymen for their political beliefs or religion. It's ironic that free thought would be suppressed in a place where a hundred years ago Goethe was fighting with his pen to remove Napoleon's forces off German soil.

By December, a new evening roll-call was staged each day, and as soon as the snow came to Ettersberg you could feel the icy wind through your thin prison clothes. There wasn't an occasion without a fatal accident being reported, and a man freezing to death on parade or being shot by a Guard when trying to run away would be such an example.

No prisoner would have tried to escape at all if he'd known the SS guarded the forest. Only one prisoner had managed to do so because he worked on a detachment outside the main guarded area. His name was Peter Forster and earlier in the year during May he had managed to shoot one SS guard dead and escape not only Buchenwald, but Germany too. His freedom was short-lived.

With the help of the Hungarian government he was captured in Budapest, arrested, and escorted back to Buchenwald.

Four days before Christmas, with specially erected scaffolding, Peter Forster was hung in front of us all as a warning to anyone planning to escape.

I stood two hundred yards from the gallows as 'Lageralteste' Richter put a rope around his neck and watched a heroic life come to an end. For two days the dead body was left hanging in the gallows while we were forced to march past it.

The power of the criminal prisoners reached a climax on New Year's Eve 1938. My friend and I saw the Kapos coming and going with bulging overcoats (the Kapos were the only prisoners allowed to have an overcoat), and they were clearly had something to hide. Their headquarters were in Block 45 which had been the last erected at Buchenwald and very well situated out of view – although close to us.

At 4.30 p.m. 'Lageralteste' Richter organised roll-call and was anxious to get it over with as quickly as possible. All the working parties arrived on parade punctually and it was all over in 30 minutes. The roll call of the same 15,000 prisoners had lasted 6 hours the previous week, during which 60 prisoners had frozen to death that one evening.

Our own New Year's Eve was spent much like any other evening: a meagre meal of bread and margarine and long before the sirens for second lights out had sounded, we were mostly fast asleep.

Then some of us were awakened by peculiar noises from outside. We were used to all kinds of sounds at night, from trigger-happy guards firing above our huts trying to frighten us, to loud screams from prisoners who threw themselves against the electric fence (for us to see in the morning).

But this was different. If the SS canteen had been closer to us we wouldn't have given the noises a second thought. From the laughter and songs, it was obvious that people were celebrating and having a New Year's party.

It was only when our hut leader drunkenly crept into his bed in the early hours of the morning that we realised it wasn't the guards who had celebrated the end of a miserable year with laughter, songs, champagne and schnapps, but the criminal prisoners.

Beneath their overcoats the Kapos had somehow managed to obtain and smuggle in some alcohol.

'What a party we had!' grinned the hut leader. 'The guard? We gave him cigarettes and a bottle of beer; we felt sorry for the poor soul.'

Next morning the roll-call was again taken in record time, and the hut leader who had a hangover didn't even bother to appear on the parade ground. He knew the Commandant was much too tired to appear, and of course the SS Guard who took the roll-call knew all about the party the previous evening.

So the mystery was, how did they get this alcohol? Exactly a month later we found out as on February 1, 1939 a delegation from Gestapo headquarters in Berlin arrived in Buchenwald, and this time Heinrich Himmler himself was paying us a visit.

Himmler had acquired a great deal of publicity since he became Minister of the Interior. The first time I saw this baby-faced Frankenstein was when, as a foreign correspondent in 1936, I watched a demonstration of the Fascist Youth Movement in Berlin.

In common with every other journalist there, I had the impression that Himmler was a harmless provincial schoolteacher. I believe he enjoyed immense power by virtue of his position in the Third Reich, but, nevertheless, shrank from using that power to the full.

This time I saw Himmler the circumstances were very different. It was a bitterly cold day and before he arrived, we had to get up earlier than usual.

After the roll-call, names were read out of those who had to report to the front gate immediately after the parade.

By 9 a.m. I was working near the electrified fence and from this position I could see twelve of the criminal prisoners standing near the gate. It was obvious they were in for some kind of punishment, because they were positioned outside the confinement cells.

An hour later, two huge Mercedes limousines arrived and stopped at the gate. Himmler, his adjutant and personal staff got out.

Shortly afterwards in the presence of Himmler and Camp Commandant Roedel, the luckless prisoners were given 25 lashes each. When one of Himmler's staff took part in inflicting this punishment on one prisoner, I could see Himmler's Satan-like face grinning horribly. This was the real Himmler at work.

Twenty-four hours after the Gestapo delegation left the camp, all the criminal prisoners involved in the Block 45 party on New Year's Eve were summoned to report at the main gate with their few belongings. It was 4.00 a.m. and still dark when they were pushed into two waiting lorries and sent to Flossenburg an even worse concentration camp than Buchenwald.

Only after their departure did the whole truth behind the alcohol at the party come to light.

All the good teeth, rings and watches the criminals had taken from the Jews who arrived in November had been converted into small gold bars, which had been hidden under the floorboards of Block 45.

Shortly after Christmas, some of the bars had been exchanged for alcohol by the leader of the SS canteen who took them to Berlin and sold them to a jeweller.

But the jeweller informed the Gestapo, who quickly discovered the source of the gold. When Himmler learned about this 'great gold robbery,' he was furious. Not because of the brutality of the criminal prisoners had used when they assaulted and murdered the Jews for their possessions, but because the gold had not been delivered to the State. Several SS officers were also recalled to Berlin and never seen again. No prison camp in any dictator state had ever witnessed such a 'drink' party as the one the criminals of Buchenwald had thrown to celebrate the start of 1939.

The reign of the criminal prisoners had suddenly come to an end. The New Year's Eve party had been their downfall.

The inner administration of the camp was now taken over by the political prisoners.

The New Year began with rumours about the release of racial and political prisoners. The 'November Jews' as we called our fellow prisoners who were still in a special compound and not assigned to any working party, were the first ones to be released, provided their relatives could prove they would leave Germany more or less immediately.

I was again transferred to another working party. The transport of dead bodies to Weimar had stopped for the time being, and I once more worked as a woodcutter outside the main camp.

One of my new working partners was an Austrian Baron named Popper. I helped push his wheelbarrow from one site to another, and saved him from exhaustion and possible death under the guard. He constantly said, 'I will never forget your assistance.'

Twelve months later, when we were both at liberty in England, the Baron was living the high life in London while I was in a transit camp on sixpence and a stamp to write home once a week.

When I wrote to him asking for some assistance, the Baron sent me a hundred cigarettes and two bars of chocolate!

Back in Buchenwald, I waited anxiously for news from home, but each time a letter arrived it was censored so I didn't know whether my mother had arranged any emigration for me, and if so, where I would go.

Shortly before Hitler's 50th birthday in 1939, I completed one year as a prisoner. The number of Jewish and political inmates who were released had increased. It was the first sign of the secret negotiations between Nazi Germany and Soviet Russia for the forthcoming non-aggression pact that was signed in August that year.

I began to lose hope of ever leaving the camp. Then, one morning at roll-call, an announcement crackled over the loudspeakers: 'The following prisoners will go immediately to Post 2, where they will be freed.'

Suddenly all 15,000 of us alerted, and the same question flashed through all our minds: 'Will I be among them. Will my name be called?'

I couldn't believe it when it was.

'Treuhaft, Gerd. 8880. Born 10.4.18. Place of birth: Berlin...'

I wanted to shout: 'I will be freed!' Instead, as in a trance I turned to my companion and said, 'Karl, take my bread bag, there is still some bread and syrup in it; and under my bed is a pair of slippers. May they bring you luck.'

Those were the last words I spoke to my companions in sorrow.

Those of us whose names had been called out stood to attention at Post 2 and watched our not-so-fortunate fellow prisoners marching off in their working parties.

Later came a medical examination.

'Any scars or wounds or other injuries?' asked the SS doctor.

'No, Herr Doctor!' For who would dare jeopardise his future freedom at this moment?

Twenty minutes later we were in the luggage store, where

each of us changed out of the striped prison uniform into civilian clothes.

Not far away from us, one of the labour gangs was hard at work, but to talk with them would have been dangerous. However, as soon as the warder's back was turned, I heard one of the prisoners say to one of our group: 'Mother will soon get my papers in order.' Not daring to say anything because of his obvious emotion, the freed man nodded.

Later he told me it was his brother.

The Oberscharführer told us of the kindness and clemency of the Führer from whom our pardon had come. Then he turned threateningly to the Jews among us and muttered, 'I should like to add to those of you leaving the country that if you ever say anything to the detriment of the National Socialist Germany, do not forget our arm is long...'

One by one the pardons were handed out and we all had to sign a paper saying we would never talk about or write about what we had heard or seen in the Buchenwald camp.

As we were climbing into the bus waiting for us outside the main gate, the first working parties were wending their way back. We drove past them, but they did not look up.

Finally, we reached the last sentry-post and the prison officer who had accompanied us, jumped out and left us.

The chains had been snapped and a new life was, unbelievably, beckoning.

It was midnight when I phoned my mother from the station at Berlin.

'I'll be home in twenty minutes,' I said breathlessly.

As I put the receiver down, I thought, for just a fleeting moment, that I might be able to blot out what had happened in the past 13 months.

But I knew that would be utterly impossible.

It was something that would be with me for the rest of my life.

Chapter Four

My mother had aged noticeably during the 14 months I had been away. She blamed herself for what had happened to me.

'I should have let you emigrate when Hitler invaded Austria, but I thought nothing would happen to you,' she kept telling me.

However, now that I was free, a great relief came over her, and we had to make plans for the future.

Although I was free, there were some nights when I would shout out loud: 'Advance for roll-call...' and, 'Left, right, left ... caps off! ... eyes right! Caps on! Straighten up!'

There was still an obligation to report to the police station in Grunewals Strasse after I returned home, but despite being a bit nervous about this they hardly took any notice of me.

We contacted one of my cousins who had emigrated to Florida a few years earlier to see if he could arrange a way out of the country, and my mother also had managed to arrange a visa for a transit camp in England, at Richborough in Kent.

At that time, the political situation in Berlin had become much more dangerous. Twelve months earlier, it was the Sudeten Germans who were crying for help from the Führer; now the Free State of Danzig wanted to be incorporated into the German Reich and the newspapers were attacking Poland.

My schoolfriends, who had all reached the conscription age, had either just finished the labour camp or had joined the army. After Dachau, my circle of friends had certainly shrunk. They were either afraid to be associated with an anti-Nazi sympathiser, or a Jew, or had joined the Nazi party to save their own skins.

Only one, Horst Dehneke, who lived in the same street and had joined the army, visited Mother on many occasions when he was on leave.

Horst and I would never forget how we escaped the infamous 'Night Of The Long Knives' back on June 30, 1934.

It was a Saturday evening, and the two of us decided to visit a night bar called the Tingle Tangel. But as soon as we walked through the front door and saw the bar was jam-packed with storm troopers, we hurriedly left and ended up at another bar further along the street.

We hadn't long been there when we heard the wailing of police car sirens outside. We didn't take much notice, much preferring to listen to the pianist who was still playing American jazz tunes.

It wasn't until the next morning that we found out the Tingel Tangel bar had been raided by the police, the Gestapo and the SS.

All the storm troopers present had been arrested and packed off to prison while a number of their leading members had been shot.

Horst and I realised we had had a very lucky escape; something that brought us closer together. It was with great sadness that I learned, when the war had ended, that he had been killed in Stalingrad. (Horst's father was an officer who had fought in the First World War and was a distant relative of the famous pilot Manfred Von Richthofen.)

Soon I was on the move again, but this time on my way to real freedom. Exactly a year after arriving at Dachau I was back at Berlin station to catch a train to the Belgian border.

My mother and I were crying because we knew that we

would never see each other again. We hugged and hugged each other until it was time to for the train to leave. I'd only been back home for four weeks.

Two Gestapo men followed us onto the train and kept and eye on a group of refugees who had joined the passengers.

At the German border control, a customs inspector looked at my small case and asked, 'Is this all you have?' I said yes, and he then asked, 'Have you been in a concentration camp?' I nodded.

'Well, don't bother to open your case. It's okay.' That was a lucky break, and such a difference to the rest of the group who were abused while emptying their luggage.

Once we had left the border, we opened the compartment windows and yelled Scheisse! (Shit!) at the top of our voices. We felt as free as birds that had just been released from their cages.

We were in high spirits through Belgium and France and then, when we crossed the Channel and approached the White Cliffs of Dover, I remember Emil Ludwig's book on Napoleon and how he had escaped from from St Helena.

There was, of course, no comparison with our situation, but being just 21 years old and having just left a horrible regime and imprisonment behind you, I couldn't help feeling that one day I would return as a conqueror.

On arrival in Richborough, Kent, at the Lord Kitchener transit camp, I couldn't help thinking when I first clapped eyes on the huts that this was another concentration camp, minus the electric wire.

It was a former First World War army base, and a Major Clark invited us into a large hall where he gave a welcome speech. He said we should be thankful to the British government for giving us asylum, and suggested that we shouldn't try to mix too much with the local people. To be honest I was disappointed with what we were being told. Our movements were going to be very restricted and at first

51

I wondered whether I had made the right decision to come. It seemed the Home Office had given instructions that refugees like me should be kept out of London and not allowed to take a job without special permission. World War Two hadn't even begun.

Later, in the dining room, I recognised lots of faces I had seen in either Dachau or Buchenwald, but those famous personalities from Block 6 in Dachau who had promised me heaven and earth if we should ever leave the camps alive, were noticeably missing.

I learned they had managed to live in London and, doubtless, had long since forgotten all about me.

In Richborough, we were given sixpence a week allowance and a first-class stamp to write a letter home. I certainly could have done with some financial help. Most of my colleagues were non-political refugees and some of them were waiting for the US permits and others had friends in England who had applied for working permits on their behalf. As soon as their permits came through, they were off.

I remembered some English friends I had met at the 1937 International Youth Conference in La Courneuve, and I managed to contact them. There was Valda Horton in Harrow, Middlesex, and Dorothy Thornton in Wales. They had both written to me in Berlin and because they never received a reply, assumed I must have been arrested for my political activities before Hitler occupied Austria.

They were both delighted to hear from me and that I was in England. Both visited me at Richborough and invited me to their homes, but before I could go I had to get the necessary permit.

Dorothy's father, a director of the Anglo-Iran Oil Company, met me at Paddington station and accompanied me to Neath, in South Wales. He paid all my expenses and made me very welcome in his home.

I stayed there for ten days before returning to camp, and

then I spent two days at Valda's home in Harrow. Valda, a schoolteacher, was a member of the Labour Party and was very anxious to help refugees from the Nazi oppression.

Having tasted this real freedom, life in Richborough became even more depressing. With the sudden death of my cousin in Florida, it now looked as if any possible stay in America was hopeless.

The political uncertainty in world affairs, with Hitler preparing his attack on Poland with the consequence of the outbreak of the Second World War, reflected strongly on the daily life at Richborough. Many refugees still had relatives living in Germany and Austria.

When, on September 3, 1939, the inevitable happened, the nerves among the camp inhabitants were at breaking point. What would happen to our families and friends who weren't able to leave Germany and Austria in time?

Even our refugee status changed overnight with the outbreak of the war: we had become enemy aliens. We were classified like members of the Nazi Party who had visited England and hadn't managed to go back in time.

Now we were not allowed to leave the camp at all, although a week later, a few concessions were made.

Shortly after the outbreak of war, I wrote to the Czechoslovakian Embassy in London to offer my services to the newly formed Czech Legion that was going to operate in Paris. However, because I wasn't a citizen, my offer was turned down.

The only war service my fellow refugees and I were allowed to do was to fill sandbags.

At the same time, a special camp for women was set up alongside ours, separated by barbed wire. Husbands were only allowed to visit their wives for two hours a day.

It was about this time when I received another invitation from Valda. But before I left camp, I was called to a special tribunal that was to classify refugees into three groups: A, B and C.

A was for Germans and Austrians who had been surprised by the declaration of war and were sent to an internment camp. B was for Germans and Austrians who were recognised by the Home Office as refugees but had to report to their local police station and were not allowed to accept work. C was for friendly foreigners who had only to report to the police if they changed their working place or domicile. The C category would be free to move for the first six months. Austrian and German citizens were still recorded by the Home Office.

A few days after the tribunal, we had some important visitors to the camp: the Archbishop of Canterbury and some members of the House of Lords. They wanted to acquaint themselves with the fate of us 3,000 refugees and they pointed out that the Allies were not fighting against the German people, but against the Nazi dictatorship. And they added that in the fight against Nazism, we refugees could possibly play an important part.

After the visit, the camp was full of rumours and speculation about the formation of some sort of international brigade or 'Foreign Legion'.

'They will never send us abroad,' said one hut leader. 'They know that if we were captured, we would be tried as traitors and shot.' And another asked, 'Are we going to become British citizens if we join the British army?'

One of my friends told me, 'If the British government is prepared to arrange through neutral countries to get our relations out of Germany and Austria, then I'm prepared to join the British army.'

Other said that we should join anyway, to show our gratitude to Britain.

There was talk of the formation of the Auxiliary Pioneer Corps, but before this came into being, I had made up my mind to join the army.

When the Auxiliary Military Pioneer Corps (AMPC) was

54

formed, we were told that after serving in it for six months, we would be able to join a fighting force, and we presumed that we would then become British citizens.

Before taking the oath of King and Country, I accepted another invitation from Valda to visit her in Harrow. It was the first time I had seen London at war. I was surprised at the number of young men in bowler hats and carrying their gas masks in the City. It was as if nothing had happened in the world. Only gas masks and the blackouts reminded us that there was a war on, but for the theatres, cinemas and restaurants it was business as usual.

It was that period which, later on, was called the 'phony war'.

In Berlin, six months before the outbreak of war, I had seen more men in uniform than in London, months after the declaration.

Was the ironic proverb that the English would fight to the last Frenchman really true? You could have believed it because there appeared to be little anti-German feeling anywhere.

I decided to visit Fleet Street, the famous home of the big English newspapers and see if I could interest any in my experiences in Dachau and Buchenwald. However when I called in at the *Daily Telegraph* I was told: 'It is all very interesting, but we cannot publish your story. Our readers wouldn't believe it. It would seem to them to be mere anti-German propaganda.'

Not only did the British press refuse to publish anti-German contributions after the outbreak of the war, but also the BBC refused a suggestion of mine to imitate Hitler's voice in broadcasting anti-Nazi speeches at the same time as he was addressing the German people.

However, three years later, they did adopt some of my ideas of psychological warfare. Sefton Delmer introduced it with the support, in *The Spectator* magazine from Harold

Nicholson. It all came about in my letter, 'Can you hear me, Heinz?' which was published in that magazine.

Back at Richborough, the main topic of the day was whether to join the army or not. Some refugees were, in fact, already in uniform but worried that they weren't to be allowed any weapons.

'What will happen to us if Hitler invades Britain and we can't defend ourselves,' I heard one say.

'We shall all perish,' replied the foreman!

Life in the camp was made all the more difficult when a number of huts were closed for renovation in readiness for the new army intake.

Those who had joined up enjoyed better food and, as new recruits, received the princely sum of fourteen shillings a week. Those who still dithered about donning a uniform had to survive on their sixpence a week allowance.

'If you are six months in the Pioneer Corps, you can be transferred to a fighting unit,' the Camp Commander told me after I had mentioned I would like to join the RAF.

So, at last, I had decided to wear a uniform once again, but this time not a dishevelled one, bearing the Star of David, but a proud one to do battle with the barbarians who had destroyed my youth.

On December 19, 1939, I swore the Oath to King George VI and his successors, unaware that just six months later, my service in the AMPC would condemn me to almost five years of peeling potatoes, cleaning lavatories and making tea.

Chapter Five

Six weeks before Christmas 1939, most of the refugees at the Kitchener Camp in Richborough had changed from civvies into khaki. For many, this quick transition was with very limited training or experience, and it surprised me how overnight people were able to become Sergeants and Lance Corporals.

We began to enjoy our new life although many of us were wondering if we were real soldiers, equal to those seen on the cinema newsreels being sent to France with the British Expeditionary Force (BEF).

On our first pay-parade we received fourteen shillings, which was a great improvement on the sixpence a week we got as refugees.

We felt as if a miracle had happened, and soon were spending our new-found riches in a café at the nearby town Sandwich, run by a Mrs Kimber.

When Christmas arrived, Lord Reading (founder of the AMPC) came to the camp. We were served traditional turkey dinner and given 20 cigarettes each. The Lord even came round our tables asking if we had any complaints. It was such a stark contrast to the previous Christmas when 20 prisoners were frozen to death. In fact this was like a fairy tale and for a moment it felt as if sunny days were here to stay.

During the first two weeks of the New Year we had marching exercises without weapons. Lord Reading had promised that we would not bear arms, as the AMPC was a labour company. However rumours began that we might be sent overseas; we couldn't understand why we hadn't had any weapon training.

One morning we prepared for a very important inspection by a special visitor Field Marshal Birdwood who was 80 years old and still working at the War Office. We were the First Alien Pioneer Corps of the AMPC and standing on parade in full army dress and with steel helmets pressing on our heads we felt like real soldiers.

In the distance we could see our friends in civvies who didn't want to join the army looking like lost sheep.

We could also hear the commandos being shouted at from all corners of the parade ground. It felt like being on a Hollywood film set, but instead of a director shouting 'Action Please' it was a Sergeant yelling 'Attention! Eyes Right.'

Field Marshal Birdwood inspected the solders and stopped from time to time to ask where we came from.

'From Berlin' said a soldier next to me.

'I knew Berlin, it was a wonderful city,' replied the Field Marshal.

A few minutes Lord Birdwood stopped again and asked a new recruit how he liked England.

'I was born in Vienna,' replied the soldier, as his knowledge of the English language wasn't up to much. Lord Reading smiled and the Field Marshal continued his inspection.

After this important visit, rumours about our possible movements began again and a Second Alien Company was formed. It was widely thought we would be sent overseas despite Lord Reading's promise that we would not be armed or put in any direct contact with the enemy.

Several Corporals and Sergeants, whose wives where billeted in the camp, tried to get a transfer to the new company hoping to stay longer in Richborough, but on January 20, 1940, we received our last orders here and they were for us to pack our kit and be ready for 4.30 a.m. reveille.

It was a bitterly cold morning, but the hall at the Kitchener

Camp was alive with people. We were to be on the move at last.

We assembled in orderly fashion and marched through the little town singing 'Roll Out The Barrel!' and 'Hanging Our Washing On The Siegfried Line'. We were heading for the local railway station.

I don't know whether we were singing for joy or from the fear – or from the uncertainty of what lay ahead.

Lord Reading and the whole staff were at the station to give a short speech and say his goodbye in German, 'Auf Wiedersehen'.

Once on the train, we found the carriages warm and very comfortable. There was also as much food as we wanted, so we had no complaints.

Outside, the lovely countryside sped past and after about six hours we arrived in Southampton. We couldn't believe our eyes. It was going to be France after all.

Here at the harbour we saw our first real scenes of war – soldiers sleeping on the ground with kitbags as pillows and with dirty uniforms. It looked liked the war had already been going for many years.

By contrast we looked smart, with our neat uniforms and highly polished boots.

A ship to Cherbourg was already waiting for us and we were soon on our way. On arrival, all I could see was British soldiers. It looked like there were no French people around at all.

We went by lorry on a short journey to the railway station that had long been neglected. Here stood endless rows of shabby, dirty old trains with no windows. Here we were given a meal – Irish stew. It was a dish we were to become very used to. Then we were squeezed into carriages, eight men to each one, and began what felt like a mystery journey.

As the cold, windowless train pulled away, we sat close to keep warm. Here I was with my comrades, all grand men.

I had known them from prison and the concentration camps. We all knew there were to be tough times ahead, so we coined a slogan 'Uns kann nichts mehr erschuttern!' that meant, 'Nothing can frighten us any more!'

Hours passed before we saw another town. We stopped for a short break somewhere in a field, and still nobody knew where we were or where we were going – but from time to time we saw big posters showing the French and British Empires saying 'nous vaincrons parce que nous somme plus forts' (we shall win because we are the strongest).

After about an hour's train journey, followed by a march through cold and deserted streets, we arrived somewhere on the outskirts of Rennes.

We were so tired we didn't ask any questions, but we did look at each other when we saw we had to sleep on the floor. We couldn't believe it!

We thought we would only be staying here for a few hours, but when the staff began building a kitchen we knew we were to set up camp and be here for a while.

Our supper was corned beef and cake. The accommodation was a run-down warehouse that had been poorly transformed into barns for Spanish refugees.

A fortnight later I wrote in my diary, 'Two weeks have passed and so many things have happened. The Kitchener Camp, which was a very basic refugee camp, seems like a paradise to us now. For beds we lay on the floor on straw, and there were no lights, chairs or tables. It was like we were living as animals.'

Now we began to get nervous. The officers didn't know what to do with themselves or what to say to us. To improve our mood and the whole atmosphere they started a pay-parade.

On our first off-duty day I walked into Rennes, an impressive place, but clearly at a time of war as people looked depressed. I went with my friends Harry and Erwin in the hope of finding proper food and warmth. The NAFFIs (army canteens set up for British soldiers) were the only place we could get English cigarettes and besides this we had a chance to exchange our shillings into francs.

Outside French soldiers and schoolboys whispered in our ears 'Any cigarettes to sell?' as they were willing to pay the price but forbidden to enter any NAFFI to buy anything.

The goods were exclusively for the BEF and of course officially we were not allowed to sell anything bought here. The Red Caps watched every move we made.

On the way back we went into a pub opposite the famous Marshal Foch barracks and, for the first time, came into contact with French soldiers.

They offered us drinks and their cigarettes, but we couldn't stomach their 'Gaulloise', the smell was enough to put anyone except a Frenchman off. Instead, we offered them some of our 'Craven A', an English brand and you could tell how pleased they were. It didn't take long before we had a circle of French soldiers around us, holding out their hands. Their average age was between 30 and 40 years old, and some of them had seen the last war.

One said, 'I've been in Germany with the last occupation army, but I tell you if I see another German I'll break his bloody neck.'

Another said, pointing to his bayonet 'If I see a German, I'll stick this into his guts. They killed my father in the First World War, and now they're trying to kill us. They are murderers. There are no good Germans, don't fall for that nonsense.'

My pal next to me didn't understand French but, understandably, became anxious to leave the pub.

After all, they thought we were British, but we came from Berlin. I was the only one who could speak a little French and, from time to time, I translated into German. But I was careful to use some dialect so that the Frenchmen thought I was English.

At 9 o'clock the bugle sounded for roll-call from the French barracks, and we all left the pub.

'I am glad you knew some French,' said Erwin. 'Otherwise we might not have got out alive.' When I translated that the French had called Germans 'bastards' and wanted 'to kill the lot of them' he felt even more terrible and we walked back to our camp feeling depressed.

Two days later we started to work – emptying sand lorries. The usual corned beef and tea was served up as lunch, and we froze each way on the open lorries travelling there and back. At first the work seemed easy, but it got much harder when it started to rain.

The organisation worked very badly and when even an officer had to wait 20 minutes for a cup of cold tea we could understand why he didn't do anything to improve conditions.

Then a flu epidemic struck the whole company and we were all sick, but no doctor came to see us. For a couple of days I was left lying in blankets on a stone floor.

From time to time a medical orderly gave me a couple of aspirin, but once I reported sick a medical officer took one look at me and, without asking any questions, said I was okay for duty.

I could hardly believe it, so I wrote a letter complaining to the Major and, without sealing it, handed it to our Sergeant Major to forward.

But he opened it, read it and barked: 'This is treason on active service. You can get sixty days detention for it!' Then he destroyed the letter and threw me out of the office. It was the first time I came into contact with the King's Rule.

I have never forgotten that episode, especially when I recall that we were fighting for freedom.

Three days later, I had another confrontation, this time with the Quartermaster Sergeant. I asked him if I could exchange my boots because they were hurting. He looked angry and shouted: 'Stand to attention when you talk to me! And call me Sir!'

I smiled and replied softly: 'Well, you too are only a refugee. Sir, can you exchange my boots?'

He went very red and, without saying another word, exchanged them.

In the meantime, the first palliasses had arrived, and we tried to organise some beds. We still had only one water pipe for two hundred and seventy two men. Nevertheless, we tried to make it a bit more homely after having slept two weeks on a stone floor.

But no sooner had we done that than the Second Alien Pioneer Corps turned up and for some reason we were ordered to give up our comfy beds to them. So it was back to the stone floor for us. Clearly the officers of the Second Corps were more concerned about the welfare of their soldiers than ours were.

The time passed quickly and the town provided plenty of entertainment. In spite of the misery at the camp, we spent some happy hours in Rennes. I came in contact with French Sergeants and officers of the French Air Force. One Sunday afternoon two French officers came with their car to the camp and invited me to join them on a visit to a dance hall.

The next day, after my CO saw the French officer saluting me, he remarked that he didn't like his soldiers having any contacts with the French – despite them being our allies. He also pointed out that the dance hall at the French coffee house was for 'Officers Only' when he found out where I had been.

I explained that the French Captain had told me 'You are my guest and I am a member of the BEF. I'll take the responsibility and ignore the notice in the window.'

A few days later I met the grand nephew of Marshal Foch and members of the 'Croix de Feu' who saluted each other with a Hitler salute.

63

I asked them why didn't they serve in the French army, and was told:

'Fighting for what? We would fight against Russia, but never against Germany.'

They were to become the advance guard of the Fifth Column that was responsible for the eventual fall of France.

At the end of February we moved to another working place, and this time we had to sleep on an old train wagon with 12 of us to each truck. We were the richest army in the world and had to live in trunks (we thought at the time). We also found out that officers had moved into comfortable hotels.

This was the period known as the 'Phony War' but discipline was still strict with punishment handed out for even the smallest piece of waste paper left lying around.

Then there were the endless helpings of the infamous Irish stew. On more than one occasion it was off and smelt terrible, and when one of the soldiers remarked that the food was better in Dachau, he was immediately confined to barracks for 14 days.

Another man wrote to his wife about the conditions in France, but it was opened at the company office and the luckless writer was given 28 days' detention in the Fortress of Brest.

In March 1940, the First English Pioneer Company joined us. They looked as if they'd all been sent here from Dartmoor Prison to complete their sentences. They seemed far less prepared for their new surroundings than we had been, and they were less disciplined.

On one occasion a Sergeant of ours (and friend of mine) lost his stripes for bad behaviour and was transferred to the English company as a Corporal. When I went to visit him I was shocked by how empty his hut was. I learnt that anything that could be sold was exchanged for cash to pay bar debts from the previous weekend's drinking.

What a difference this was from the behavior of our company who were lawyers, doctors, solicitors and well-known businessmen. Some of them had even served in the First World War and had been decorated with the 'Iron Cross' for their courage. A move from our company to theirs was considered a demotion.

By the end of April, Rennes was predominantly occupied by British troops. Wherever we went, there were Red Caps who would shouts at us to take our hands out of our pockets or pull our garters up properly. We couldn't understand this kind of warfare and we all hoped there would be some action soon.

The next big event in our lives was a move into Nissen huts, which were clean, comfortable and well lit with paraffin lamps. After our previous accommodation in France, we all agreed that we wouldn't mind staying here until the end of the war. We each had three blankets, but we had barely settled into this new luxury when Hitler invaded Norway and Denmark.

Some of my friends had relatives who had emigrated from Nazi Germany to Denmark and Norway. Naturally they wondered what would happen to them.

I had a cousin who until now had forwarded my letters via Holland to my foster mother in Berlin.

Later I learned that he was sent to the gas chambers with his wife and two-year-old son.

When we asked our officers about what was happening, very little interest was shown in their response. All we were repeatedly told was, 'We are going to push the Germans back. Don't worry.' They were referring to the invasion forces of the Third Reich who were advancing into Norway and Denmark.

One day we marched to our working place where Herbert and I were in charge of the field kitchen and my job was to collect the water from the local farmer.

At the same time I had the opportunity to listen to the radio and inform myself and my friends about the latest news on the front.

Returning from the farm I reported to my friend that I had just heard on the radio that the King of Belgium had surrendered.

'This is impossible, you must be mad, you can't have heard this!' said the Sergeant and added, ' Your French isn't so good that you can translate radio news into German or English.'

At first the whole company stopped working with the shock of this news. However when the lunchtime editions of the *Daily Mail* and *Le Matin* appeared with no mention of the King, nobody believed me any more. Only news of the King fighting on the Albert canal was mentioned and I was told that I couldn't have heard properly.

In fact a Sergeant said, 'I shall report you to the Major for spreading horrible news. You are going to be in trouble, you may even be sent to prison for spreading false rumours.'

Then, two hours later, after leaving work we met newspaper boys shouting 'extra' to editions of *Le Matin* and *Paris Soir* with the headlines 'The King of Belgium has surrendered'.

At the same time there was a tense atmosphere growing in Paris. The government of Prime Minister Reynauld wasn't at all popular. The arrest of left-wing supporters and members of the former Leon Blum government gave the anti-war movements and Fifth Column organisers encouragement to surrender to the Germans.

Back at the camp I got into trouble again. This time for writing to a French girl Yvonne I had met at a dance in Cesson. I had sent a letter saying I would have to cancel our rendezvous as the rumour was our company was to move again.

The letter, which I wrote in French, was intercepted and

our Captain questioned me about the King's Rules and Regulations.

'Are you reading the daily orders posted at the company office?' he asked.

'No Sir,' I said. 'My knowledge of the English language isn't good enough.'

The question was repeated in German and I got a telling off for once again mixing with the French. The first of May wasn't celebrated in the camp. When I passed the company office whistling the Internationale, the Corporal in charge yelled: 'Stop that whistling, you Bolshevist!'

'You'll be glad if the Bolshevists came to our assistance one day,' I shouted back and continued whistling. It didn't take long for the incident to be reported to Major Priester.

Without knowing it at the time, I was immediately marked down as a Communist in the Major's eyes, even though I had never been a member of any political party.

But the Major regarded most of the refugees from Germany and Austria who had opposed the Nazi regime as being either Communist or a left-wing supporter. For just expressing an opinion, a promotion for me was now out of the question.

On May 17, 1940, Hitler invaded Holland and Belgium and the atmosphere in our camp reached boiling point. Rumours that 15,000 bombers over Germany had returned home safely, and that 10,000 Nazis had drowned in the River Marne were supposed to lift our spirits, but the news direct from London and Paris gave a different picture of the situation.

Now the King of Belgium had surrendered to the Germans, Hitler entered Paris without any military resistance at all. Soon we began to hear explosions just a few miles away.

Then the Royal Engineers suddenly blew up the railway crossing for the new station we had been building, and we began to wonder what was next in store for us.

The great tragedy of Dunkirk had finished, and the Germans were moving into Nancy and Rennes. Passing the camp we saw long trains loaded with barbed wire, while outside there were long queues of cars trying to escape from the Germans.

We were still doing the same work we had done when we arrived five months ago, but on the afternoon of June 14 we were told to load barbed wire from the great depot of Rennes back into trucks. We did not know where it was going to be sent – back to England or to the front.

It was then the Royal Engineers blew up the railway crossing for the new station we had spent so many Sundays at work and for two days we felt very apprehensive. Hardly anyone spoke as hour by hour we sensed the Germans approaching.

We still hadn't been issued with weapons, and we began to wonder if it really was going to be concentration camp for us a second time. We all tried to find the civilian clothes we had brought with us from England. Perhaps our only hope was to escape to the South of France. Our faces were pale with fear.

Suddenly, at about 3.00 p.m., we were given the order by an orderly corporal. We were told to leave all kitbags and overcoats in the huts and pack a few belongings. Twenty minutes later we were packed into lorries and taken to the railway station. The people of Rennes gave us a great cheer as we left, as they thought we were the second BEF – though in reality we were frightened.

After what seemed like an eternity waiting, the train started to move in one direction – with endless trains loaded with tanks heading in the other.

It was five o'clock the next morning when we arrived in harbour town St Malo. We were dead tired but glad to be further away from the enemy.

We marched into a large square in the middle of the town where we met all the Alien Companies and a few British regiments.

We could see in the eyes of the officers that a great battle had been lost and they did not know what to do next.

Many before us must have escaped from this place, and I have never seen such confusion. New cars, uniforms and gas masks were all lying around and even the food stores had not been emptied, so we ate and drank our fill. Perhaps these would be our last hours.

When the order came that we were to board a ship and that no personal belongings were allowed, we exchanged our last civilian clothes for French wine.

As we marched to the ship singing 'Kiss Me Goodnight Sergeant Major,' a large crowd had gathered, quiet and orderly. A few voices cried out, 'Come back soon!' Meanwhile, France was putting her signature to capitulation.

We were detailed into two small boats, and some of us tried to get near the lifeboats, just in case. I slept throughout the whole night, and when I awoke, the Captain told us that France had collapsed.

Now England was in sight and, after a journey lasting 22 hours, we arrived in Weymouth. It was a pleasant seaside town, full of happy smiling people, many of whom gave us ice cream and sweets.

You would not have known there was a war on.

Chapter Six

After disembarking at Weymouth, many of my refugee friends sent telegrams to their relatives who had moved to England. However nobody knew at the time that, since the Nazi occupation of Holland and Belgium, the Home Office had given an order to 'Intern the lot'. This was a particularly controversial move on behalf of the British, and even affected relatives of members of the British forces.

I had no relatives to tell that I had arrived safely.

Two hours later we were once again sitting on a train. This time it was more comfortable but we still didn't know where we were going. At each station we passed people who were clapping their hands and waving to us as if we had come from some victorious battle.

Occasionally through the windows we saw, to our complete surprise, men of our own age group playing cricket and tennis. We just looked at each other with the same thought: 'Haven't they realised the seriousness of the situation?'

It was almost midnight when we arrived somewhere in London. You couldn't see the station because of the blackout, but we later discovered it was Victoria.

We climbed wearily into waiting coaches, again not knowing where we were heading. Now we didn't care so much as we were out of the reach of the Nazi army – which it transpired had entered Rennes just two hours after we had left.

Once out of the coaches, we marched through the empty London streets and stopped outside a very impressive building.

'This is the Empress Hall, and you'll be staying here for a couple of nights,' explained the Sergeant in charge. We could hardly believe it. It was very grand.

Inside, there were rows of tables covered with neat white cloths. We could smell the food that had been prepared for us. In between each table, were mattresses.

It was an enjoyable stay even though we were not allowed to leave the Hall without permission. Only four men from each section were granted a permit.

After a short propaganda march through London on June 22 we were off again, this time on a train to Devonshire, to the Westward Ho holiday camp, now headquarters of the AMPC.

Waiting to greet us on arrival was Lord Reading and his adjutant. What a reunion! Six months earlier, he had bade us Auf Wiedersehen at the Sandwich railway station, and none of us could possibly have realised we would be back so soon following the defeat of France and a retreat from Dunkirk.

At Westward Ho we met old friends from Richborough and during the two days we were there we caught up on each other's news and gossip.

Then we were off to Bideford where we noticed that the first daily order on the notice board read: 'German speaking is strictly forbidden. If anyone is caught speaking German, his weekly pay (fourteen shillings) will be stopped immediately and he will be put on kitchen fatigue for a week.'

'Are we fighting a war against Mozart, Schiller, Beethoven or Goethe?' I asked the Sergeant when he later tried to stop a German conversation in our tent.

I reminded him that Lord Reading and members of the House of Lords had no objections to our using our mother tongue.

'Remember, even Neville Chamberlain had declared on the September 3, 1939 that we were waging war not against the German people but against Nazism,' I added.

71

From Bideford, we were given our first army leave. Many of my friends who were anxious to visit their relatives in London were surprised to find that most of them had been interned on the Isle of Man as 'enemy aliens'. It was paradoxical that a father, brother or cousin of a member of HM Forces was behind barbed wire in the same camp as a prisoner of war.

On July 7, 1940, I wrote in my diary: 'I have been to London on 48 hours leave. The city hasn't changed much since I spent a few days there last November. There are still young people not in uniform who think the war should not interfere with their daily routines and business. However the news that Russia has invaded Bessarabia and Bukuvia is welcome in the city.'

My leave passed too quickly to make any contacts with Fleet Street Editors, but this was going to be high on my agenda in the future.

Back in Bideford a new exercise with borrowed rifles had started, and the daily order of 'German Speaking Is Forbidden' was still in force.

Four of my friends had spent their two-day leave in Sandwich, checking up on private luggage they had left behind before leaving for France. They were told that a Polish army unit returning from Dunkirk had broken into the luggage store.

'Where was the British Military Police?' they asked. The atmosphere in the company had reached its lowest point since we were evacuated from St Malo.

At the end of July, a hundred soldiers myself among them were detailed to another Devonshire village to put up tents.

On arrival, the authorities were surprised to see so many of us. They had, apparently, asked for ten men not a hundred.

We made the job last two weeks by having a very easy time playing cards and enjoying the summer weather.

The Battle of Britain hadn't yet begun. It was the time

when Hitler, having conquered France and invaded the Low Countries, was still hoping Britain would surrender.

We seemed to be on the move all the time, and we next found ourselves in the castle at Dillington Park, near Ilminster in Somerset. Well, I say 'in the castle', but that was reserved for officers only. The men were billeted in stables, garages and tents, each with three blankets and a straw mattress.

We were actually treated like second-class citizens, only allowed to leave camp every second Sunday, and only then if we could prove we were going to the cinema.

When the Major received an anonymous letter complaining about the treatment and conditions, we were all immediately confined to barracks.

Specimens of our handwriting had to be submitted to the company office, but the Major never did find out the culprit.

A new English officer, who had served a number of years in India, arrived and thought we were all his slaves. He inspected the working parties every day and told the sergeants to watch our movements very closely.

I received the first news from my friends who had not joined the Pioneer Corps and who had been sent to Canada and Australia. In a Red Cross letter, Hermann Sprecher, who had travelled with me from Berlin to Richborough and who had suffered in a concentration camp, told me he was now interned in Canada with German prisoners of war.

The letter was the talk of our camp, and many of us began to doubt the principles for which we were fighting the war.

I sent a letter to the known pro-refugee paper, the *Manchester Guardian* which was published under the heading Refugees:

'Sir, a few days ago I received a letter from a friend in Canada who writes: We are getting on all right, food and treatment are okay, but the damned barbed-wire narrows our life terribly.

'Twenty-seven months ago, he and I came to England together after having been through the German prison and concentration camps. After the outbreak of the war we went together before a tribunal and were put in category C.

'I joined the Pioneer Corps and my friend had a visa for the United States and intended to go there.

'I went to France with the B.E.F., but my friend remained in the refugee camp waiting for the opportunity to cross the ocean.

'When in May 1940, my friend was sent to Canada for internment, it surprised me that two people who had fled from Nazi Germany for identical reasons should find under British legislation two totally different forms of treatment.

'Thousands of refugees who received the C qualification are interned in Canada and Australia. If this qualification is not sufficient for the government, why not form a new tribunal and allow refugees who are still interned to go before a fresh examination?

'The procedure would release many to help Britain in her war effort. If the released refugees are in Canada or Australia, let them go as free men into munitions factories. After two years, surely we know who is a refugee from Nazi oppression and who is a secret Fifth Columnist. Sincerely, J.G. (Josef Geta).'

For the first time, Members of the House of Commons and the Fabian Society tried to contact the Ministry of War to ask that British citizenship should be granted to soldiers serving in HM Forces.

I was given a new job at Dillington Park: organising the water supply from a nearby farm.

For the first time I came into contact with a typical English family at war and, to my surprise, there was no anti-German feeling.

The farmer's wife kept saying, 'We can't condemn a whole nation for a madman like Hitler.'

She was a keen piano player and very fond of Austrian and German composers. Her daughter Diana was even anxious to learn German (she later joined the Control Commission in Germany).

I visited the farm during my off-duty hours, and Diana's mother always gave me cakes, fruit and chocolate to take back to the camp.

With the start of the Battle of Britain, gossip and arguments about our treatment by the officers and the Major were overshadowed by current events. We saw the Junkers and Hurricanes flying over Somerset and once we heard a bomb dropped at the town of Chard.

Twenty-five years later, when I met Emmy Goering in her flat in Munich, she told me that Hermann didn't want to destroy England, he wanted to make peace with your country, but Hitler and Goebbels wanted a total victory after the collapse of France.

Watching a dogfight in the skies above us was one of the most incredible sights to us at Ilminister as the days went past. Meanwhile I took the opportunity to improve my knowledge of the English language and subscribed to a number of journals, including the left-wing *Labour Monthly*. It condemned the police of Home Secretary Sir John Anderson who, when referring to Jewish refugees from Germany, had said, 'Intern the lot.'

My possession of left-wing publications from London caused another confrontation with the Major.

One day, the Orderly Sergeant told me that while I was out with a working party, the Major had inspected the tents and spotted copies of *Labour Monthly* and *New World And Review* next to my kitbag. He had commented that I must be a Communist, and as such might be a danger to company morale.

I was furious about the accusation and arranged an interview with the Major.

'You wanted to see me?' he said as I entered his office. 'What about?'

'I hear there are rumours that I am a Communist,' I said. 'I would like to say that I have never been a member of any political party or trade union, but I am certainly an anti-Nazi and have no sympathies whatsoever with any right-wing organisations.

'I am a Socialist and I thought England was a democracy where I could freely express my political views.'

The Major looked at me for a short while and then replied, 'Your political views are of no interest to me as long as you refrain from making propaganda in the company.'

And he added, tapping me on the shoulder, 'Maybe I am a Socialist, and if anyone in the company tries to insult you, you should report it to me.'

The incident was closed and rumours about my political views stopped. But I didn't know what the Major was really thinking. The comments he made in my personal file were locked in the company's safe and were only re-opened two years later.

After eleven months' service, I received my first two weeks' army leave. I went to London and stayed in the YMCA, spending days sightseeing and the evenings in different dance halls.

There was the Astoria or the Paramount in Charing Cross Road; the Hammersmith Palais and Covent Garden where the Opera House was then transformed into a dance hall.

It was while I was on leave that I received a telegram informing me that the company had moved from Dillington Park to Bexleyheath in Kent, where I was to report on my return.

The Battle of Britain had come to an end and now the Luftwaffe concentrated their attacks on London. We were all billeted in separate private houses near the railway station and, like clockwork, we could hear the air-raid sirens regularly at 6 o'clock every evening and the 'all-clear' between 9 and 10 o'clock.

The following days we had to clear the bomb damage, each section of the company competing with the other to work efficiently.

The Major and the officers were very pleased with our work and the people of London were wonderful. Knowing we were Jewish refugees from Germany and Austria, they provided us constantly with cups of tea, cakes and cigarettes. Some invited us to lunch or dinner to share their meagre rations. There was no anti-German feeling.

And so my first year in the army came to an end, and it was very disappointing to still be treated as a second-class soldier who had responsibilities but precious few rights.

Then came the December 29, 1940. It's a day I'll never forget and a story of mine that has been published many times since...

Another Blitz night was over, and long before reveille was sounded we prepared ourselves for the usual Sunday trip to London.

By the time the Orderly Sergeant came from house to house banging on doors and shouting in his Prussian voice 'Get Up,' there was already the customary queue each morning outside the House Sergeant's own house waiting for our daily passes.

The sirens sounded the 'all clear', but we knew that by 6.00 p.m. the Luftwaffe would come again.

The earplugs we were all issued with were used by very few of us. The noises through those winter nights couldn't rob us of our sleep. Outside the booking office at the station I recognised my section comrades by their voices along with boys from the HQ and the kitchen.

Never had this small station, which was only 40 miles from London, seen so many soldiers. The noise of their studded boots gave the impression of a whole regiment on the move.

As soon as the train moved you could hear the usual

Sunday morning conversation going on all around. The Saturday evening dance was the topic of all discussions.

For the first few seconds of listening you would have been shocked. These men in khaki didn't speak English or even a dialect spoken in one of the Dominions. If you listened carefully you would have realised that what you were hearing was the language of the pilots who dropped the fire and high explosives bombs on our district. Yes, it was German – the language of the enemy being spoken right here in the coach.

Perhaps these were German prisoners, you might have thought. Then you would observe they were wearing khaki and their gas masks were covered with the tin hat similar to that of a Tommy.

By the time we reached Charing Cross station some lonely English passengers returning home from a Saturday evening out, or from night duty, knew we were members of the First Alien Pioneer Corps in Great Britain.

Nearly 90 per cent of us had been in concentration camps before coming to England.

The West End of London was still sleeping. On all street corners you could see newspaper men sorting out their first batches of Sunday papers.

There was only one restaurant open, Lyons Corner House in the Strand, and even at this early hour, there was a queue outside. And a most unusual queue it was, too.

These people were half-dressed; very few had had a proper wash and under their arms they held a couple of blankets, or young children, or both. Some slept, some cried – the Underground was their only home.

For hours they had queued to get a sleeping place at the station, and now they wanted a cup of tea.

It was a scene I was to see often and is still one of my lasting impressions from those Blitz days.

On those Sunday mornings, some of my colleagues visited

relatives in other parts of London, but I usually walked to Hyde Park where the first speakers had already taken their places.

They talked of liberty, freedom, right and wrong. They defended and accused Soviet-Russia and of course the pacifist speakers were there too. But the more I listened, the more I came to the conclusion it was like Much Ado About Nothing.

On this occasion, I was surprised to bump into an old friend, Hans. The previous week he had quarrelled with his girlfriend and didn't want to go back to her, so we strolled to the nearby YMCA and chatted over a cup of tea.

I had known Hans from Berlin where we went to the same school and we chatted about the good old days when we were young.

We arranged to meet up that evening at Lyons. I also planned to take Lily, who I had met a few days earlier at a dance hall at the Astoria.

When we arrived, Hans was already there, eating with a girl by his side. It hadn't taken him long to find a new partner.

When the bandleader announced that the alert had just sounded, nobody took any notice, but Hans looked at the time and said, 'We'd better go, don't you think?'

I agreed, but just then the band started to play one of my favourite tunes, 'J'attendrai,' so I told him, 'I'll be with you in a second, I just want to listen to this song.'

He nodded and said that he'd pay his bill and his new girlfriend was going to see him off at the station. 'I'll see you at Waterloo,' he added.

When the band had finished playing, I paid our bill and Lily and I walked towards the exit.

Suddenly a firebomb landed about 100 yards from the restaurant, causing people in the street to scramble into the entrance for shelter. We couldn't move.

79

It was mayhem in Charing Cross Road and we had great difficulty in reaching the station from where I hoped to get a bus or train to Waterloo.

'Sorry, no trains for the next 20 minutes,' came the announcement over the platform speakers. I looked around hoping to spot Hans, who must have caught the bus to bring us back to Bexley but he was nowhere to be seen.

There was the sound of bombs all around us and neither Lily nor I realised that London was going through the heaviest night of the Blitz.

My only thought was what would the Major say? I had just finished my first year in the army and had never yet been up for punishment.

As Lily and I sat on the tube stairs hoping it would soon be over, another loudspeaker announcement told us there would be no more trains that night.

'If only I hadn't stopped to listen to that last song,' I said to Lily. 'What are we going to do now?'

'Come home with me,' she suggested. I had known her for little more than a month, and wondered what her mother would say, but as there was nowhere else to go, I accepted her invitation.

As we walked to her home, bombs were still dropping uninterruptedly around us.

Lily's mother made me very welcome, gave me a cup of strong tea and showed me to the room I was to share with Lily's younger brother.

As I drifted off the sleep, the words 'court martial' went over and over in my mind along with 'close arrest' and 'pay stopped'.

I rose at 6 o'clock with the rest of the family, had a good breakfast and caught the first train back to camp.

On arrival I saw the Orderly Sergeant riding towards me on his bicycle shouting that I was to report immediately to the company office.

Now I was for it, I thought, as I knocked on the Major's door.

'I am so glad you are here,' he said as I entered, and held out a hand to shake mine.

'So am I,' I replied, bewildered, because this was not the reception I had expected.

Then he asked me if I had had enough sleep and did I want to go straight to my billet for a couple of hours rest.

I left the office confused, but soon I realised everyone thought I'd been killed.

'What happened?,' I asked the Orderly Corporal.

'Don't you know? A bomb fell on a bus and eight of our men have been killed.'

'Hans too, I'm afraid,' he added, knowing from another friend that I had been with him in the afternoon.

The song 'J'attendrai' had saved my life, and so again I was glad to be alive.

Later that evening we sat around the fire in our room listening to the BBC news. At the end, the announcer repeated these words: 'Remember, remember the 29th of December...'

At the beginning of the New Year, the Major was replaced by a new commanding officer, who was wearing an RAF badge on his uniform.

I recalled that, before joining the Pioneer Corps, the recruiting officer at Richborough had promised us that, after six months' service in the Corps, we could apply to join any unit in the army, navy or air force.

So I immediately applied to be transferred to the RAF,

'Why do you want to join the RAF?' was his first question, 'And which unit?'

'Bomber Command, sir,' I answered.

He smiled because he had just come from Bomber Command to our unit.

'Have you any relatives in Germany?' he asked.

'Yes, my foster mother is in Berlin, but not having heard from her in months, I don't know if she's alive.'

'Any relatives in England?'

'No, sir.'

'What would you do if you were on a bombing mission to Berlin. How would you feel about that?'

'If it would help to shorten the war, then it would be my duty to do it.'

'What if you have to bail out and are taken prisoner?'

'The Nazis will never get me alive again, sir. A second time in a concentration camp is out of the question.'

He nodded and promised to forward my application to the War Office.

A little later there were rumours circulating that an Austrian Legion was going to be formed, and that we would be separated if it became officially recognised by the government.

The former Austrian ambassador Baron von Frankenstein, Count Starhemberg and a certain Mr Allina were the sponsors of the Austrian Legion, but most of us in my section were against the idea and had no intention of joining it.

I drafted a memorandum under the title 'Austrian Legion – What For?' pointing out that even among the Austrian refugees, there wasn't a political party that would justify the formation of a Legion.

I sent a copy to Vernon Bartlett, a well-known journalist who was Foreign Editor of the *News Chronicle* and also an MP for Bridgewater.

He was known for his extensive knowledge of Central Europe and the German language. I asked him if he would kindly forward the memo either to the War Office or Foreign Office and, if possible, raise a question in the House of Commons.

A month later, during my second army leave, I went to London and, not having heard from Vernon Bartlett, decided to visit him at his newspaper in Bouverie Street.

He wasn't in, but I saw his secretary who told me that he had, in fact, replied two days earlier, and she showed me a copy of his letter.

To my great surprise, Vernon Bartlett had not only sent my memo to the War Office and Foreign Office, but had raised the question in the House. I was delighted and thrilled that a memo from me was to be discussed in parliament.

It would have been good to have thanked him in person for his interest in the Pioneer Corps, especially as I also wanted to give him a manuscript I had written with my friend Heinz Feldheim about our experiences in the concentration camps.

Heinz had spent four years in the concentration camp and was released from Buchenwald a fortnight before me, then emigrated to England. He was interned in May 1940, and after his release joined the Pioneer Corps. We had written a book about our experiences in Buchenwald that I left for Mr Bartlett together with an article I had written under my pen name 'Josef Geta'.

The article had been published in Darlington's co-operative journal *Wheatsheaf* and was the story about the brave Pastor Schneider.

It was late in the summer of 1938 when nearly all English newspapers reported the death of Pastor Schneider in the concentration camp of Buchenwald.

Only in London was there a special remembrance service. Like thousands of compatriots he suffered under the Nazis, but generally he was not well known.

I never met him in Buchenwald, but remember an episode at the time in the camp that portrayed the real courage of a man who died for his ideal. It was either the end of March or beginning of April. I don't know the exact date as we never knew what day or month it was in the camp.

It was about 5.30 a.m. and the SS man, who counted us in lines each morning, told us he had an announcement.

Dead silence hung over the Square when suddenly we heard a voice from the Bunker Cell where Pastor Schneider was kept.

Schneider had never seen the daylight since he'd been there, and it was with a fleshless hand that gripped the iron-grilled railings of the bolted window that he broke the deadly silence with his words:

'Don't follow those murderers. They are scorning the Command of God. Thou shalt not kill. God will punish them. I have been kept in the dark cell. I am innocent. My only crime is that I am a Christian and I believe in God.'

Now his voice was getting fainter and unintelligible. Roedel, the commandant of Buchenwald, was furious. He rushed to the window to beat the prisoner with his stick, but the window was too high up to reach the prisoner's hands. The Pastor Schneider continued until he sunk exhausted and disappeared from the window.

When the roll-call was over that day and we were lined up to go to our working parties, the Pastor's speech dominated all conversation inside and outside the camp. The SS Guard was told and soon all of Weimar knew about it, but we never saw Pastor Schneider again.

Vernon Bartlett contacted me to say he was very impressed with my story and promised that he would forward my manuscript to the publisher Victor Gollancz, but it was without success.

Before I had started my army leave I had also contacted Mr John Parker MP, member of the Fabian society (later to become Lord Parker) for an interview that he granted me. I told Mr Parker about the difficulties in the Pioneer Corps, the treatment we had received from the Sergeant Major, and the army order stating that we were not allowed to speak German – even in our barracks and among ourselves. I mentioned that I had also made an application for a transfer to the RAF.

Before returning to my unit at the end of my leave, I also paid a visit to Mr Allina, the Austrian who had the intention to form an Austrian Legion inside the British army under the slogan 'Free Austria'.

Herr Allina had a very impressive office in Eaton Square and as I arrived in British army uniform he gave me a good reception. He told me of the importance he felt in forming an Austrian Legion, but this was not what I believed in. When I told him that I had written to Vernon Bartlett with a memorandum against such a formation, and that Bartlett had submitted it to the Minister For War, Sir Anthony Eden, Mr Allina was not only very surprised but tried to persuade me to change my mind and submit a new memorandum to the War Office via my contacts with John Parker and Vernon Bartlett. I refused, and a few months later a club under the name 'Austrian Centre' was formed.

On the last day of my army leave, June 2, 1941, Hitler invaded Russia and overnight the British Communist Party changed their attitude towards the war. It was no longer Imperialistic, but a war of liberation and Winston Churchill shook hands with the British leader of the Communist Party, Harry Pollitt.

Now I thought my application for transfer to the RAF might have a better chance of being successful.

During my leave in London, where I also spent time with Lily – who had just enlisted in the WAAF – our company moved yet again, this time from Bexleyheath to Darlington.

The Quaker town had a very peaceful atmosphere and the people were quiet and reserved. Our new quarters were in a former factory building where, after dark, the rats and mice would have themselves a rendezvous. It was called 'Free Man's Place.'

We got a new Company Sergeant Major who, for reasons best known to himself, decided to treat us as if we were still in a concentration camp.

However, I wanted to write contributions to *Die Zeitung*, a German newspaper published in London, and I knew I had to be nice to the Major to get his permission to do so. Members of HM Forces were not allowed to write letters or contribute articles to any newspaper or journal without the permission of the commanding officer.

At first he was hesitant, but then he agreed on condition that I submit all articles to him to be forwarded to the Colonel for final approval before giving them to the newspaper. Of course I agreed.

Then came the good news that I was being called for a meeting with three RAF Officers concerning my application. I was hopeful because I knew my friend Erich had applied and had already been given three interviews.

Erich told me that during his first interview alone with the Major, he had been given the name of a well known factory in Germany and asked if he knew where it would be on a map. When he saw the map he couldn't believe it as the map was from pre-war 1914! Was this the best information the RAF could come up with?? We were both stunned.

He was also asked if he had any relatives living in the district and if he was willing to fly there on a bombing mission.

During my own interview the RAF men asked me some general questions that I answered easily and they seemed to be impressed. Then the Major, who had been standing by, whispered something in the ear of one of the officers and suddenly their attitude changed.

'I am very sorry Private Treuhaft,' one of them said. 'You are short-sighted in your left eye and we cannot accept your application to join the RAF.'

I saluted the officers and left the room.

When I returned back to my section my friend Harry joked, 'What's the problem? You can still see perfectly well out of your right eye!'

86

However I wanted to know what the Major had said to the officers so later that day I asked him privately. The Major leaned back in his armchair and replied, 'Sorry, you have no chance of getting my approval to join the RAF. You are a Communist and your report in my file says you read *Labour Monthly*.'

I was speechless. And then I remembered my incident with the previous Major in Dillington Park.

'Yes, I do read that magazine, but it doesn't mean I am a Communist,' I replied. 'I also read journals like *Time And Tide*, *The Spectator*, the *New Statesman* and *Nation*. We are living in a democratic state. Aren't we fighting for free speech and freedom of thought?'

'We don't like left-wing elements in the RAF,' was his reply.

After this official interview we had another thirty minutes' discussion about current affairs. During this conversation with the Major he also said to me, 'Your English is very good. The daily order is that German speaking is forbidden, so as this doesn't affect you why do you want to stir up trouble?'

I explained to him that the older members of the company still have difficulties explaining themselves in English, as they haven't mastered the language yet.

'As long as I am the CSM in this company I am giving the orders even if the whole company doesn't like it,' he replied.

The following day, when I met the Duty Corporal, he mentioned my long interview with the Major and said, 'Gerd, the Major was very impressed with your knowledge of current affairs.'

But I didn't like his attitude and so I wrote to Vernon Bartlett and John Parker about the interview.

It was about this time that our sadistic Sergeant Major punished one soldier by making him wash the windows of Woolworths in the main street of Darlington wearing his full uniform, complete with steel helmet and gas mask when the temperature was in the 80s.

When passers-by asked the Sergeant Major how could he treat a soldier in that way, he simply smiled and told them, 'Don't be upset. He isn't a British soldier. He's German.' The soldier afterwards complained to the Major and got the reply: 'You should be proud to be a German.' It completely ignored the fact that the soldier was married to a Pole who had disappeared in the ghetto. The complaint was dismissed.

When I later requested another interview with the Major because I intended to take up a correspondence course with the London School of Journalism, he immediately asked if I knew a Mr Vernon Bartlett, and, if so, who was he?

I was surprised that the Major hadn't heard of the well-known journalist, MP and broadcaster.

'Yes, I know Mr Bartlett,' I replied.

The Major then asked why I wanted to see him.

I told him about the London School of Journalism and that I wondered if I could have some financial help to join.

The Major agreed to lend me £5 on the understanding that I repay him five shillings a week. I then asked him what had happened to the articles I had given him months earlier for him and the Colonel to read before submitting them to *Die Zeitung*.

He opened his drawer, and there they were. He still had not given them to the Colonel, but he promised to do so and then send them to the Editor in London.

The daily routine in the Pioneer Corps didn't change much and we followed the war on the Eastern Front through newsreels and newspapers.

When, on December 7, 1941, Pearl Harbor brought the United States into the war, we knew Nazi Germany had no chance of winning it. The political refugees, who didn't join the army and were now released from the Isle of Man, started to become more active. The Austrian Centre became a meeting place for Jewish and non-Jewish refugees.

Dr Emil Maurer, who I had known from the concentration camp in Dachau, was leader of the Austrian Labour and Trade Union in exile. Refugees from Austria were more popular than those from Germany. Their pre-war Ambassador Baron von Frankenstein was not only well known in the diplomatic circle, but had arranged Viennese evenings in London with great success. This was unlike the last German Ambassador, Herr Joachim von Ribbentrop, who when giving his diplomatic credentials to King George V at St James's Court greeted him with the Hitler salute.

After seven years in exile, the German anti-Nazi movement had not been able to form a government in exile like the Czech and Polish Refugees. British politicians on both sides of the House of Commons claimed that the political refugees from Germany had lost contact with current events inside Germany and that the German culture club and the Free German Youth movement, which was formed after the outbreak of the Second World War, in London were communist inspired.

The German Karl Hagen formed a 'Neu Beginnen Group' hoping to form an opposition in exile but he refused members of the former Weimar Republic to join him. These included Hans Vogel, the former member of the German Reichstag; Erich Ollenhauer; Victor Schiff who was working for the *Daily Herald*; and Hans Gottfurcht, former member of the German Trade Union.

The group met once a month at Broadhurst Gardens in West Hampstead for a discussion about the future of Germany, but there was no unity in the group. The German emigrant, Bernhard Menne, supported the view of Lord Vansittart, who had published a book called *Black Record* condemning all Germans claiming there were no good Germans at all.

He recalled the events of June 30, 1934, 'The Night of

the Long Knives,' which gave us a warning of the Nazi regime. Now even the former friend of Hitler, Gregor Strasser was campaigning against the Nazis from his place in Canada. The 90 per cent of refugees from Germany and Austria were Jewish and most had no intention of ever returning to Germany or Austria.

The small group of political refugees from Germany, who had refused to join the British army because they where afraid to become traitors to their country, had organised a money collection from their supporters – who had joined the army to assist their aims.

My friend Martin Meyer, a former member of the Social Democratic Party, who had spent years in prison and concentration camps for his political conviction, was in charge of collecting the contributions for the SPD in the army. When on July 17, 1940 the company daily order said that speaking German was forbidden and English lessons after working hours were made compulsory, I asked Martin to contact the SPD members in London. They had contacts with the Members of Parliament and I requested they raise the issue in the House of Commons. But his friends weren't successful.

At that time I was attached to the Regimental Police and on night duty so I had enough time to work on a memorandum under the title 'Is the German language a danger?' which I sent to Members of the House of Commons and to Lord Wedgwood.

At the beginning of 1942 the War Office issued new orders stating that members of the Pioneer Corps could now volunteer to serve in fighting units abroad, but only 30 members out of the 250 applied for one, and they were all newcomers who had joined the Pioneer Corps after Dunkirk.

Two weeks after the new instruction from the War Office the Major asked me for an interview.

'You can now join the fighting forces, Treuhaft,' said the Major. I asked him if the status 'enemy alien' would disappear

G.T. in his army days

G.T's Press Card

PRESS

G.T's United
Nations Public
Relations Press
Card

G.T. with Dane Clark and Margaret Lockwood. *Highly Dangerous,* Pinewood
Studios 1950

© J. Arthur Rank Organisation Ltd

Richard Basehart on the set of
The Intimate Stranger

© *Associated British Picture Corp. Ltd*

Merle Oberon, wife of Sir Alexander
Korda, filming *The Price of Fear* in
London 1956

G.T with Horst Buchholz the 24-year-old German box office star in his first
English role in the film *Tiger Bay*, 1958   © The London News Agency Photos Ltd

INGRID BERGMAN

G.T. with Ingrid Bergman filming *Indiscreet,* Elstree Studios 1958

© *Associated British Picture Corp. Ltd*

G.T. with Van Johnson while making the film *Beyond the Place*, 1959

G.T. with Richard Todd and Michael Anderson on the set of *Never Let Go*, 1960

G.T. with June Ritchie making the film *A Kind of Loving,* 1961

G.T. with Maurice Chevalier

G.T. with Richard Attenborough

Left to right: Mrs E. Herzog, G.Treuhaft, Albert Cohen and Jean Simmons on her 21st birthday, Mrs Herzog has just presented Jean with a cookery book

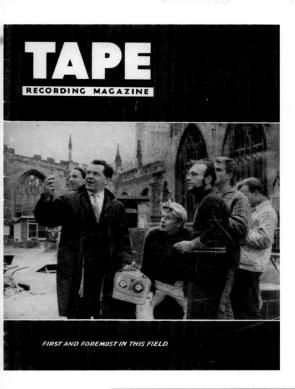

G.T. talks to a party of Germans who are helping to rebuild Coventry Cathedral

G.T. with Elizabeth Taylor

G.T. with John Mills at the Berlin Film Festival

G.T. with Phyllis Calvert

G.T. with Marta Toren while making the film *The Man Who Watched the Trains Go By*

G.T. with Mara Lane

G.T. with Nadine Tallier
© *Associated British Picture
Corp. Ltd*

G.T. with Nigel Patrick

G.T. with Sylvia Syms

G.T. with Van Heflin

G.T. interviewing Walt Disney

G.T. with Claude Rains while making the film *The Man Who Watched the Trains Go By*

G.T. with Hildegard Knef

G.T. with Gert Froebe

G.T. with Elke Somme

G.T. with Sophia Loren

G.T. with Eartha Kitt while making the film *Chastity Belt* at Elstree Studio, 1971

G.T. with Francis Durbridge

G.T. with Tony Martin
(singer/star of *Meet Me in Las Vegas*)

G.T. with Doug McClure and son Ralph and co-star

Family photo from left to right: Gerd, Ralph, Helen and Joan

for members of the forces who applied for a transfer to a fighting unit, but the Major didn't know.

When a member in the House of Commons raised the question with Ernest Bevin who was responsible for the Home Office he declared that the status of members of the Pioneer Corps who were going to be transferred to a fighting unit outside the United Kingdom had not changed.

'As long as I am classified as an enemy alien I have no intention to be transferred to a fighting unit except to the RAF to which I had been turned down,' I told him. The Major leaned back in his armchair and said, 'Have you forgotten what England has done for you? Where would you be if you hadn't joined the Pioneer Corps?'

'In Canada, Sir,' I replied, at which point the Major ended the interview.

The atmosphere in the company became more difficult for me but I still had permission to write short features for the Darlington journal *The Wheatsheaf*.

On September 19 I sent a contribution in the form of a reader's letter to the well-known weekly publication *The Spectator* about the negative attitude of the anti-Nazi propaganda in the BBC. I wrote it under the heading 'Can you hear me Heinz?'

My suggestion was not only published in *The Spectator*, but the well-known English Diplomat Harold Nicolson mentioned my suggestion in his leading article. He said, 'Josef Geta's suggestion should be studied and taken seriously.'

On October 1 I received a letter from the BBC inviting me to come to London and explain my suggestion of psychological warfare. Again I needed a special permit from the Major for a 48-hour leave, but when he read the letter from the BBC and my published contribution he said, 'You knew the rules. You are not allowed to write to the paper without my permission.'

However I received my pass and visited the BBC in

London. Here I met the Programme Editor and explained to him that an effective anti-Nazi propaganda should be directed to a person or special organisation like the Hitler Youth, The NSBO, the Nazi Trade Union and not just to the German people as it has been done previously. That was the reason why I called my contributions, 'Can You Hear Me, Heinz?'

Four weeks later the BBC adopted my suggestion but I never received a fee or any acknowledgment. To my surprise journalist and broadcaster Sefton Delmer on his radio transmission from Calais also later adopted the idea.

On my return from London I was transferred from my police duty at my section. Something had happened in the company, and when the CSM asked me if I knew John Parker, MP, I said, 'Yes I knew him.'

'Is he a member of the Communist Party?' asked the CSM, and I had to smile at his lack of knowledge about current affairs.

'No, Sir, he is the chairman of the Fabian Society and Labour MP in the House of Commons.'

Now the CSM said to me in a threatening voice, 'If any member of this company approaches an MP without the knowledge of the Major he can expect two years' detention.'

The CSM had tried to intimidate me, but after having survived Dachau and Buchenwald I wasn't afraid of his threat and I replied, 'Whoever has written to the MP will certainly survive two years' detention.' Annoyed he left the room.

Two days after my argument with the Sergeant Major, he received a copy of the following letter from Sir Edward Grigg from the War Office. It said 'Dear Mr Parker, you wrote to Captain Margesson on the 14th August and 4th September about members of the Pioneer Corps who have been forbidden to talk in German. Even though it may be in certain cases considered a hardship that loyal aliens should not speak a foreign language in public, it is necessary for security reasons and in their own interest. When they are in

His Majesty's uniform they should speak the King's English. Also it is bad for discipline for other ranks to speak German in the hearing of Officers or N.C.Os who do not understand the language, yours sincerely...'

The Major had received the letter directly from the War Office, and the CSM was furious that I, a Private in the Pioneer Corps, had direct contacts with the War Office without consulting the Major.

The nights were drawing in and the atmosphere in the company didn't improve with the arrival of two new Corporals from the HQ who had emigrated to England before the war and had only served twelve months in the army.

On their arrival they had strict instructions from the Major and CSM to speak only English, although both Corporals came from Vienna. The Corporal who wasn't attached to our Section 8 had all his questions answered in German from us.

The next incident occurred when one of our comrades complained about the treatment by the CSM. He too had applied to join the RAF and was one of the first two hundred refugees who had to join the AMPC. The Major replied to his complaint by saying that he had only joined the army to escape internment.

My friend Bobby took the complaint further and saw the Colonel who declared there was a misunderstanding. Later Bobby joined the Parachute Regiment. He was killed at Arnhem.

I prepared myself for my last army leave in the 69 Company. Visiting London again. Here was one of my first appointments with Colonel Lord Wedgwood who was well known for helping political refugees from Germany and Austria.

'Is your Sergeant Major a bastard?' was Lord Wedgwood's first question when I met him at the House of Commons. I smiled and I told him about the situation and difficulties in the company. He made notes and promised to help me and to contact Sir Edward Grigg, but shortly after my meeting with Lord Wedgwood he died and I approached John Parker again.

After being turned down to join the RAF I was anxious to obtain a transfer to the Army Education Corps as I had realised it was becoming more and more difficult for me to stay in the 69 Company.

During my November leave I met Sir Edward Hulton, who was a very successful publisher with *Picture Post* and *World Review*.

A year previously I had submitted a contribution 'A Peace Plan For Europe' and was one of the prizewinners of a year's free subscription to *World Review*.

Sir Edward Hulton congratulated me and published another article. His Secretary, Miss Saxby, invited me for lunch, and in 1946 I represented the *World Review* at the First Assembly of the United Nations in London.

I interviewed the French Foreign Minister Bidault, the Czech Foreign Minister Jan Masaryk, Mrs Roosevelt and the Polish Foreign Minister. I was invited by the Belgian Foreign Minister Spaak to meet the British Prime Minister Clem Attlee.

Back to the 69 Company. After the attack on Pearl Harbor our section was posted to a small village near York. Working with the Royal Engineers we were treated like British soldiers for the first time. Our job was to lay cables for a private building contractor.

The foreman of the building company promised us a bonus if we reached a certain quota. We had been working with civilian employees and at the end of our first working day the employer gave us three cigarettes each. We certainly didn't think much of the bonus.

On Friday, the pay-day, we expected an extra five shillings. Some of us even hoped to receive a pound that would have been justified, but when the foreman of the building company

94

who had employed us gave us two shillings, we sent it to Mrs Churchill for her organisation 'Aid for Russia.'

During the second week, the employer didn't even appear at the working place, and the third week we were replaced by a British Pioneer Corps. As the new work assignment was a road leading towards an airport, and despite wearing King's Uniform, we were still classified as 'enemy aliens'.

When we returned to Darlington again, we learned that the Company had a new Medical Officer. After having been attached to our company for one week he told the Duty Corporal that too many soldiers in the company were reporting sick.

'I would send them back to Germany,' he said if they didn't like the army food and kept complaining. His comments were soon the talk of the town.

Luckily I did not stay there much longer because on February 3, 1942 I was transferred to another Pioneer Company stationed in the lovely spa of Cheltenham and surrounded by a new atmosphere.

A chapter of my army career had come to an end and a new turbulent phase was about to open its doors.

Chapter Seven

In February 1942, after leaving the 69 Company, I arrived at the Arncott Camp in Bicester to join the 251 Company. Here the people were different as members included refugees who had previously been interned in either Canada or the Isle of Man. It was a strange mix because one member had a relative who was fighting with the Germans on the Russian front; others had been evacuated from Narvik after Hitler had invaded Norway, but all of these men had chosen to join the army.

Our Sergeant Major was a little man named Machin, and I had the impression he had seen the files on me before I reported for duty. With a possible reputation for being outspoken and having contacts in the House of Commons, I wasn't surprised that one of the first jobs he gave me was cleaning out the lavatory buckets. This was even more degrading than making the tea for the 69 Company.

I was now even more determined to leave the Pioneer Corps, either through a medical discharge or through a transfer to the AEC (Army Education Corps) or perhaps the Intelligence Service.

Two weeks after my arrival at 251 Company, I reported sick, complaining about the pains in my leg where I still had very visible bayonet scars received at Dachau.

The MO prescribed eight days of light duty, but still being on so-called sanitary duty, I reported sick again and was sent to a hospital in Cheltenham.

As it happened, it was the same time that the writer Arthur Koestler was also trying to get a medical discharge from the hospital. He succeeded with the help of actor Emlyn Williams.

(I took the liberty of writing to Emlyn Williams asking if he could assist me in getting my discharge from the Pioneer Corps. He was good enough to reply, but regretted that as he didn't know me personally he couldn't interfere with army rules and regulations.)

During one inspection in hospital, the MO said that if I kept complaining about the scars on my leg, he might suggest that the leg be amputated. It was obvious he was trying to frighten me.

This period was an all-time low for me, and when I caught the flu I really started feeling sorry for myself. It was a time to reflect, and the Ward Sister was only to keen to hear my story, as I already explained at the start of this book. I really felt my life had truly ended on March 11, 1938, four years ago almost to the month and day.

So what happened next?

Well after three weeks in hospital, an army psychologist came to see me, obviously sent at the request of the MO. He was a Jewish Army Captain and when he learned I had been in Dachau and Buchenwald, he appreciated I had already endured much suffering.

'I can't personally discharge you,' he said, 'But I will talk to the Colonel and the Major.'

The result was that I was sent for a month to a convalescent home, where I gave lectures on current affairs and Nazi education.

When I returned to my company, I continued complaining about my leg, and this time was sent to hospital in Radcliffe, Oxford. Here I underwent a test that can only be described as being to see if I was mad!

Major David organised it and I had to spend an hour filling in a special paper that looked like a crossword puzzle. After having filled in the black spaces and crosses, Major David called for me.

'You did very well in the test,' he smiled. 'But I haven't the authority to discharge you from the army. But I will make certain recommendations to your Major.'

When I returned to the Company unit, the atmosphere was remarkably different. The Major suggested that I work in the kitchen and if I ever wanted to attend any lecture at Oxford University, he would give me permission. Even the Sergeant Major left me in peace.

Several of my friends were transferred to different fighting units, and one of them, Gerald Lietz, who had emigrated from Danzig, had special contacts with Sir Stafford Cripps, once British Ambassador to Moscow and now with MI5. I was not surprised to learn that Gerald had been promoted to Colonel in the secret services. (In Danzig he had special connections to Hermann Rauschnigg, once the Senate President who'd had difficulties with Hitler after he had become Chancellor. In fact he wrote a book, *Hitler Speaks*, which was translated into several languages.)

After having spent almost two years in the 251 Pioneer Company, I suddenly received marching orders to report to another Company in Blundelsand, Liverpool.

I wasn't told the reason why, and for a moment I thought about deserting. Before I was due to report to the unit in Liverpool, I popped into London to ask the advice of someone I had met there earlier – Jean Dobbs, Private Secretary to the *News Chronicle*'s diplomatic correspondent, a Mr Montgomery.

I asked her to help me decide whether I should go to Liverpool or, instead, go underground in Wales with a group of conscientious objectors I had heard about.

Jean suggested I get in touch with my friend Gerald Lietz at the War Office. I did and he said I should go to Liverpool while he tried to find out the reason for my sudden move.

On arrival in Liverpool I was put under close arrest for failing to report on time – and also for leaving my kitbag with my friends in London.

But my confinement didn't last long as the Company Sergeant Major had orders for my release pending further instructions from the War Office. It all sounded rather grand and I was promoted to Company Clerk to the Major. Not bad for someone whose previous duties so recently had included making tea and cleaning lavatories.

Working in the company office gave me more opportunities to continue with my freelance writing, especially as it happened that one of the clerks was a former Editor of the *Birmingham Post* and yet another had worked for the *Glasgow Herald*.

However a few weeks later the Major received an instruction from the WSBO (War Office Selection Board For Officers) that I should attend the OCTU (Officer Cadet Training Unit) near Blackburn. I found out that this was under the recommendation of John Parker MP (later Lord Parker), Vernon Bartlett MP and Dorothy Buxton, who thought I might be interested in being an Officer.

I wrote in my diary, 'It was raining like hell when I arrived at the nearest station to the barracks. While waiting twenty minutes for a bus, I thought of every English swear word I could think of before reminding myself that this wasn't a typical case of going to somewhere to fill in forms and be asked questions where nothing came of it. This is a good opportunity for me so I must have patience.'

At 5.30 p.m. I arrived at the entrance for candidates and was told by an ATS girl that my hut was number 21 and called 'Tobruk'. Even though we were warned not to flirt or even smile at the ATS girls, I couldn't help grinning at the idea that our quarters were named after such a grand battle. Not to mention that I'd just been in hospital in a bed next to somebody who'd be injured there.

In the hut I was soon joined by a QSM who had arrived for his second training course and didn't seem too pleased with the sleeping conditions. We left to find the anteroom where 15 other candidates had already arrived.

The atmosphere in the room was icy and at first we just looked at each other feeling a bit uneasy. I wondered how one of the men, who couldn't have been older than 19 or 20, would have looked with a pip on his shoulder. Beside him was a CQSM, an older-looking solider and I wondered whether his education and experience would be sufficient for him to attain the rank as an Officer.

Conversation between us all began very slowly, and I was too tired to take much of an active part so I went to bed early.

Reveille was at 8.00 a.m., and when I awoke I was nearly frozen. Then I had to shave in cold water, but there were no grumbles. We all knew what we were there for and we just accepted the conditions.

At about 10 a.m. this first morning we were given a written test with 100 questions. Some were straightforward and I felt I did pretty well with, despite the English required to fully comprehend them all was perhaps beyond my own standard at that time. Others were more unusual and included being asked to choose figures for a field in a book. This was a question set by a psychiatrist.

'I wonder what they can get from it,' the CQSM said. 'If they are going to judge whether I am "nuts" or not from this question, I'm sure I'll never pass the test!'

We then heard a short talk from the Colonel, a 'Blimp'-like character who looked like a caricature of David Low. He gave us a short introduction as to what we had to do, what they were looking for, and what they expected from us. It was all quite sensible and everything seemed easy.

At the dinner table we all discussed the morning's questionnaire and the Colonel's speech and, with everyone being on their best behaviour, we hardly noticed we were being waited on by the ATS.

There was no 'pass the bloody salt'. It was 'would you

101

be so kind as to pass me the salt. Oh, and I'm terribly sorry to bother you, but could you pass me the pepper too?'

I think we all felt we would make very good Officers that evening, while the Commanding Officers kept an eye out for who they felt should be recommended for commissions.

Over the next few days came more questionnaires, and to be honest I was glad when the time for being asked, 'Is your father dead – Yes/No?' was over. They just didn't seem challenging and I thought it would have been more interesting to ask, 'How has your father managed to stay alive?' or 'Which books would you choose if you were sent abroad?' I would have chosen *Why Was I Killed?* by Rex Warner; *Tomorrow Always Comes* by Vernon Bartlett; *Arrival and Departure* by Arthur Koestler and *The German Army of Today* by William Necker. This may have been a surprise to the Officer dealing with our forms who I'm sure would have expected *Military Law*, *King's Rules & Regulations* and anything by Dickens and Shakespeare.

At one of the group discussions with the Major, I sat opposite a schoolteacher. He had just joined the army, but from the way he spoke he seemed to me as if he would be far more useful in the Army Education Corps than the RA. He was very qualified in his profession and hardly of Herculean constitution.

Next to me sat Kenneth who wanted a commission in the RAMC, and was generally very active when he wasn't busy either lighting or knocking out his pipe.

We had a discussion on post-war planning of education, during which I gave a talk on Nazi education that I could see interested the Board.

All our activities went under the watchful eyes of our Captain (a Colonel who reminded me of the film actor Peter Lorre), and the Major. I watched the Major during our exercise where he hardly changed his facial expression. You could see his brain was working and nobody went unnoticed through his glasses that made his short figure look more impressive. The Major was also a psychiatrist and it was said he could tell your future from your handwriting and could read your thoughts when you spoke to him. You may get sent to an institution rather then get a commission, we used to joke to each other.

Then came an interview with our Captain who was President of the Board.

'Take a seat No. 21,' said a deep male voice when I entered the interview room. It was a friendly gesture, not given in the usual command style to which I was more accustomed. The Colonel had no 'Blimp' mannerisms, so I thought perhaps he had served in India or in the Boer War.

The way he spoke was like a teacher handing out career advice to a student he cared about, and the interview went well. He even promised me some help, which is something I had heard before where nothing came of it – though this time it felt genuine.

By now we were all getting on famously and I felt good to be a part of this wonderful group of people. The more we became friends the more it felt as if we had all known each other for years.

We had an obstacle course in which seven men had to pass a certain area and figure out how we were going to get the last man over. This reminded me of the book *And Seven Shall Die*, and I said so. Even the Captain understood the joke and we all had a good laugh.

On the final day we stacked our kitbags in the anteroom and prepared ourselves for our final interview with the Major. It was the first time we had a chance to get to know each other personally and I think he thought my background was more interesting than most of the other candidates.

I guessed he must have come from the Continent and his appearance reminded me of a former Austrian press attaché in Berlin. Still you couldn't tell this from his English.

He asked me about my parents, where I came from, and we struck up a great conversation until he asked whether I would accept a Commission in a Pioneer Corps in Africa.

'No Sir,' I replied, to which looked very surprised. I wanted to join the Intelligence Corps here in England, and did not feel I would be so useful in Africa.

It wasn't the last time I was disappointed. A few weeks later after my return from the OCTU course, the Group Commander Colonel Alexander, brother of Field Marshal Alexander, visited our unit and asked the Major that I should report to him. I thought perhaps that this was the moment I had waited for.

The Colonel looked at my file and information on my past, asked me how many languages I spoke then wanted to know what I was doing in the Pioneer Corps.

'I was hoping for a transfer to the Army Intelligence Corps, or the Intelligence Company,' I replied.

The interview came to an end and I returned to my Unit hoping that my days in the Pioneer Corps had come to an end.

But I was mistaken. The reason Colonel Alexander had come to visit me in Blundelsand here in Liverpool was because the newspapers had reported that Jessica Mitford, daughter to the Duke Of Devonshire, was going to marry a lawyer called Robert Treuhaft. Her first husband, Esmond Rommily, was a nephew of Winston Churchill and had been killed in action during November 1941.

The Colonel came to see whether the Private in the Pioneer Corps with the same surname might be related to the Duke of Devonshire.

Fifteen years later I contacted Jessica Treuhaft and received a letter back saying that she believed we must be related in some way. She added she would contact her mother-in-law hoping she would get in touch with me. Sadly she never did.

When Jessica visited London to promote her book *A Fine Old Conflict*, I met her at the Café Royal in Piccadilly Circus. She was pleased to see me and signed her book 'To Gerd Treuhaft, from old Aunt Jessica Mitford'.

I stayed in Liverpool until the Spring of 1944 when the company moved to Surrey. But the stay in this new location was not for long. In the beginning of August I was told that I was going to be released from the army on some technical grounds that they would not reveal to me, and to this day I don't know what they were.

Moreover, under conditions of the discharge, I had eight weeks before I would once again become an 'alien' without a British passport. I would have to report to the police for a new identity card and ration book.

I decided to go and see Vernon Bartlett, and he suggested I pay another visit to Sefton Delmar at the BBC.

Delmar was a well-known personality at the time, and like me he was from Berlin, though the son of an Australian Professor. He left Germany the first time in 1917 during the First World War, but returned after an Oxford education to be a foreign correspondent for the *Daily Express*. He was one of the few journalists to have interviewed Hitler before he came to power, and indeed supported the Third Reich until Neville Chamberlain had surrendered Czechoslovakia to them.

Taking more of an active role in the war he broadcasted so-called 'black propaganda' to the German people, and the last time I'd seen him it was when I had my own ideas of what should be broadcasted to confuse the German troops to try and make them surrender.

He was astonished to find me waiting on the seventh floor of Bush House in London where he now interviewed people for the BBC. Sadly he told me there was nothing he could do for me but he promised he would keep an eye out for any vacancies.

'Down again?' said the lift girl. I nodded. Yes, I was certainly 'down again' with just one week to go before reverting to my alien status.

On August 31, 1944 I wrote in my diary:

'I expected too much. Somehow I thought the doors were open and there were a just a few more steps to getting to where I wanted to be. But these steps seem endless and nothing has turned up.'

I considered my whole situation utterly hopeless.

Chapter Eight

I went looking for a job about eight weeks after receiving my discharge papers from the army. I was still curious about why I was discharged, but all my certificate said was 'Services no longer required for the purposes enlisted.'

My friends tried to encourage me by saying that with all my contacts I should have little trouble getting a job, but each time I went to the Labour Exchange I was told to come back the following week.

Then, just as the small income I received from the army was about to run out, I ran into Alfred Schoenferber, who I had not only known from my army service but also had been with me in Dachau and Buchenwald. We had been released on the same day in fact.

Alfred came from Nuremberg where his only offence was being Jewish. This had so offended Gauleiter Julius Streicher that he was sent to prison and had his shoe factory in Argentina confiscated by the Nazis. He had also served the 69 Pioneer Corps after emigrating to Britain and was discharged after two and a half years of service.

We met again in Tottenham Court Road and he was very pleased to see me. I told him I was looking for a job and he said, 'Well if you are not too proud I can offer you part-time employment as a dish-washer at "Joe Lyons" in Piccadilly. I work there and I'll have a word with my foreman.'

He was good to his word and I got the job. At first I thought it would be ideal because I could continue being a freelance journalist under my pen name Josef Geta, and being

107

at Joe Lyons would give me a wealth of ideas for human stories.

There was a Nigerian named Jim, for example, who worked in the kitchen on the second floor. Whatever time you were there, day or night, you would see him working and in the end Alfred was reprimanded for employing someone who worked more than 60 hours a week.

It was only then it became clear that it was not the same person who clocked in at 7.00 a.m. and didn't leave until the late evening. Jim had a friend called Tim who looked so similar they were able to seek employment with the same work permit. They used to swap over while clocking out and back in at lunchtime. It would seem inconceivable now, but in the '40s we were all so unfamiliar with Nigerians that it was not so easy to tell them apart, especially as Jim (and Tim) kept very much to themselves.

The casual labour at Joe Lyons always increased over the weekend, and I was amazed one week to see one of my ex-Sergeant Majors working alongside me. He'd come down to London for the weekend and needed to work to afford his fare back to Liverpool.

Soon I realised that washing dishes was not so great after all, and to make anything decent I had to work nearly 60 hours a week. It was dull, monotonous work and the hardest times were the evenings and weekends when I'd rather be doing something different.

Out of frustration I wrote a story called 'One And Eight An Hour' which got published in an army magazine. In it I wrote 'You think of the chap enjoying himself on the common with his girl or taking his "bike out to Surrey". That's when you feel really mad about the whole thing and want to break the plates one by one.

'It's on Sunday afternoon, when the streets seem quiet and most probably the sun is out, that it's worst. When three feet above me I see the filthy garbage tins overflowing with old cabbage leaves, then I really know it's a Sunday, otherwise they'd be empty.'

Not everybody at Joe Lyons worked there on a strictly legal basis, including my fellow worker Bob who came to work with a Burma ribbon on his sleeve. I knew he had another job and it wasn't allowed for him to seek additional employment, but seeing that he was I said to him one day

'Hello Bob,' I said. 'You here again? You must be coining money at the hours you're working!'

He was a big, blond, well-built fellow and replied in his native Lancashire accent, 'Not exactly coining it, just making a bob or two. But I'll be packing it in soon, I don't think it's worth it.'

'Why?' I queried.

'Well, here's how I look at it. I have to wangle in order to come here during the day; there's a hell'uva risk, and if I'm caught – well...' he shrugged his shoulders. 'I'll go over the wall. The wife allowance will be stopped and I lose my freedom to prison. So what do I gain from it? The money I've earned here will have to go to the wife and I'm right back where I started – broke!'

Bob liked to moan, but it was true that it was hard to get ahead financially. Once he referred to the kitchen as being 'even harder to be in than the jungle'!

But busy restaurants can quickly find someone else to fill a man's place, and after complaining once too many he was replaced by 'Jock' – a Merchant Navy bloke who had been torpedoed twice. Soon he was thinking the same way with the lousy pay, steaming hot working conditions and long hours of standing around watching pieces of china going round and round in a big machine. It got everyone the same way in the end.

It was noticeable that many of the staff at Joe Lyons were war veterans passing through. Some were from the First World War, but mainly they came from the war in progress

109

and in the faces of many you could see the endurance and suffering of it in their eyes. I wondered at times what they saw in mine.

I also found out that our restaurant was sometimes used as a cover for MI5 agents. On one occasion my friend 'Martin' asked me if my foreman would object to employing two ex-prisoners of war who had contacts with a spy organisation in Germany opposed to Hitler.

The two men came to work in civvies and stayed for three weeks before disappearing. This was typical of the intrigue that went with working here. In fact it's a well-known fact that Ho Chi Min washed dishes at the Joe Lyons in Marble Arch before he became President of Vietnam.

Next to ours was Regent's Palace, a more glamorous venue for secret agents who planned the future of Europe while our dishwashers turned round next door.

What I remember specifically was not wanting to be anywhere near a dishwasher in May 1945 on the day the war ended, but I had no choice and reluctantly accepted an offer of free food for the day on top of my wages to work from 11.00 a.m. to 7.00 p.m. as we served all day long with queues around the block.

The mood of the people over the next few weeks was one of great joy and elation. The war was over and people celebrated, and even I took a step back from my boring job and enjoyed the moment. In fact within eight weeks I had met my future wife, Joan.

Soon things were back to normal, and one day on my way to work I passed a small bookshop in Newton Street owned by Charles Lahr, a larger than life and controversial character who had escaped Germany in 1905 to avoid conscription. It didn't stop him being interned at Alexander Palace as an 'enemy alien' during the First World War and interned again before the Second for dealing in stolen books. He managed to get released early because of a new act in the House of Commons that allowed special conditions because he had an English wife and two daughters to support.

He had moved his shop here after his last in Holborn had been bombed in 1941, and rode his bike to work every day from his home in Highgate.

He introduced me to the work of his friend and author H.E. Bates, whose work Charles had published in his own quarterly *The New Coterie*. Bates wrote *Fair Stood The Wind For France* (1944), and later *The Jacaranda Tree* (1949) and of course *The Darling Buds Of May* (1948).

Bates also wrote under the pen name Flying Officer X for the *News Chronicle*, for which in 1943 I had a story published called 'Ten Years of Education For Death' about the Hitler Youth Movement.

In December 1945 I found out that an organisation called the United Nations was being founded and that its very first assembly was being held in January. It would have been impossible to attend this as a free-lance journalist, so I contacted Sir Edward Hulton – owner of the Hulton Press. He published many titles including *Picture Post*, *Lilliput* and at one time his father (also Sir Edward Hulton) owned the *Evening Standard*.

I had met him previously having been prizewinner of a competition held in *World Review* by writing an entry 'The Future Of Europe After The War'. The piece I wrote suggested we should have a United Europe after we had defeated Nazi Germany with Britain among its leaders.

When I contacted Sir Edward again I asked whether I could represent *World Review* at the assembly, and word came back that he would be delighted – especially as I was already a frequent contributor to the journal. One of my articles, in fact, had been published in the same issue as an interview with George Bernard Shaw so I felt I'd been in good company.

I was also to represent another magazine to which I

111

contributed – the *Central European Observer*, a London-based journal supported by the former Czech Prime Minister Dr Edward Benes and the former Foreign Minister Jan Masaryk. And so, with glittering credentials I attended three days at the first General Assembly of the United Nations conference at London's Westminster Hall from January 10, 1946. This included the reception on the first evening at Claridges Hotel where I could get to meet the delegates. It was here I was introduced to Prime Minister Clement Attlee who didn't strike me as being a great statesman, more a good school head teacher.

During the reception I also met Madame Tabouis, a much-read correspondent to the French paper *Le Figaro*. She said 'I told my readers long before the outbreak of the war that Hitler was a dangerous man and we should never have dealt with him. We should have re-occupied the Rhineland when he broke the Treaty of Versailles in March 1935.

'The Third Reich would have come to an end, and there would have been no occupation of Austria or Czechoslovakia. We would have prevented the Holocaust and all the terrible loss of lives.'

I certainly agreed with her.

When the Conference finished I returned to my job at Joe Lyons, and in-between shifts I wrote an article 'I Attended The United Nations Conference' which was published in an ex-services journal.

It read:

If the walls of the Central Hall in Westminster could recall the meetings, speeches, demonstrations and resolutions of the past twelve months – from the 'Hands Off Greece' campaign to 'Save Europe Now,' and finally the opening words of this first United Nations Conference, they would have to admit that those during the two hours on January 10, 1946, between 4 p.m. and 6 p.m., were the most impressive.

112

But an impressive demonstration with an overcrowded public and press gallery does not mean that the brand new United Nations Organisation would be a success. I have attended bigger and better organised meetings in the capitals of Europe between the two world wars in which the words Peace, Paix and Frieden repeated itself in every second sentence of the speakers. In fact hanging over this conference like a shadow was the cold, dark atmosphere of War, Guerre and Krieg.

To introduce such a terrible ghost into the Central Hall here at Westminster could perhaps be seen as unjustified pessimism, but there were already issues between the many delegates attending here, especially issues over the atomic bomb.

The first speech by the Argentine ambassador did not clear the atmosphere. Nevertheless, the delegates with whom I spoke did not share my gloomy outlook.

When I asked Senator Cyril Connally what America would do if the UN fails, he said, 'It cannot and will not fail, and don't speak of another war.'

I reminded the Senator of failures from the conferences in Casablanca, Tehran, Yalta and Potsdam, but he frankly refused to make any comments about them.

When speaking to Paul Boncour and M. Maniulski, Foreign Commissar of the Ukraine, they also declined to comment – but then it was still only the second day of the conference.

I have to say that from my short talk with Mrs Eleanor Roosevelt and Mr Stettinius, I found the American delegation among the most pleasant at the conference.

My remark to the Norwegian Foreign Minister Trygve Lie that the old League of Nations was greater than the United Nations, brought the prompt response, 'You're wrong. The United Nations Organisation will be much greater.'

113

I asked Lt. Col. W.R. Hodgson, the Australian minister to France what political and economic role Australia would play inside the UNO.

'We can play a great part,' he said. 'Remember, Australia took part on every battle front, and not only this, we took an active part in shaping the Atlantic Charter and played a very great part to achieve victory.

'It seems that too many people have already forgotten that Australia took a part towards the various economic preparatory commissions at the conference in San Francisco and towards this conference – without thanks. We even nearly failed to be elected to the economic council.

'It seems to me that the Big Five are playing the major part on all subjects and that a small country such as ours doesn't stand much chance.

'Remember, it was Australia which always achieved full employment in her domestic affairs even during the years of 1929 and 1931.'

When I spoke to the Polish Minister for Foreign Affairs, Wincenty Rzymowski, he denied that his government was anti-Semitic. He told me that General Anders and his officer corps in Italy who are fascists and anti-Jewish were responsible for the anti-Jewish wave in Europe.

'My government is helping all Jewish organisations inside Poland and no discrimination is being made as to origin or religion,' he added.

During the end of the UN conference, it seemed to me that the successor of the League of Nations is fully aware of the great responsibilities that are lying in front of it.

Not having faced the major issues of Persia, Greece, Indonesia and Spain, we must not look at the first UN conference as a failure of a mission, but the new

114

institution has had to form its fundamental bases before dealing with the above-mentioned questions.

The better world cannot be built in an atmosphere of pessimism and mistrust nor with a tremendous outburst of idealism and optimism, but by the recognition of the political obstacles in front us.

That was the end of my report.

For the months leading up to the end of this war, and around a year after, I continued to wash dishes at 'Joe Lyons', write articles where I could, and spend a lot of spare time in the library at Leicester Square reading newspapers.

Just before Christmas in 1946 I read in both the *New Statesman* and *Spectator* that a certain Henri Jourdan was to give a lecture at the French Institute in Kensington.

Professor Jourdan was my 'Uncle Heinrich' who my mother had gone to for help when I was arrested by the Gestapo. As I was not a French citizen he was unable to help, but mother kept in contact with him until the outbreak of the war.

Shortly after I arrived at the Kitchener Camp in Richborough in June 1939, Professor Jourdan wrote to me enclosing a one pound note and a message that his secretary, Miss Gumpold – who I had met in Berlin, was now living in London and that if I needed any help I should contact her. Two months later war was declared and that was the last I heard from him.

The Professor had spent the war years in Switzerland, but now he was on a lecture tour in London.

When I went to see him at the Institute he looked surprised. He knew I had survived the concentration camps but had no idea about what had happened to me during the war years.

'Good to see you,' he said, shaking me warmly by the hand. 'So what have you been up to since leaving the army?'

'Washing dishes at Joe Lyons,' I replied.

'That's terrible. Let me see if I can find you more suitable work,' he said.

To help me out, the first thing he did was to give me the keys to his London flat and employ me to look after it while he was away. He could also see I'd become more experienced as a journalist and suggested I approach more newspapers.

I took the Professor's advice and managed to secure extra freelance work that I managed to fit in between shifts at Joe Lyons.

One day I got a call from *Peace News*, who were looking for a special report. It meant that, as their correspondent, I would have to take a fortnight off work from washing dishes and take a trip.

So in January 1947 I set off by train to Dover for a short boat trip to Ostend. It was very cold and the icy weather made the journey extremely uncomfortable – it was the start of a journey back to Berlin!

Chapter Nine

Boarding another train from Ostend, I stood and looked at the empty fields where from only a few years before the Nazis had begun their bombing raids against England. After sitting down I struck up a conversation with a Belgian businessman who was on his way to Brussels.

'It's amazing how quickly your country has recovered from the terrible political and economic blows it received during the German occupation,' I said.

'Yes I agree with you. In some ways we are even better off than you are in England, if we are to believe all the newspaper reports. But also we have to thank England, the USA and Canada for the splendid help they gave us after the Germans left. The Belgian government even got 200,000 tons of wheat from Canada, although the Germans did leave behind quite a bit of food too as their retreat came quicker than expected. Today Belgium is in the lucky position of being able to buy beef from Argentina and fish from Portugal.

'Before the Second World War,' he continued, 'Belgium lived off its own products. Today, in the second year after the war however, conditions are still far from having reached the pre-war standard. The main problem is transport. During the last months of the war, too many railway bridges were blown up, and by 1944 Belgium only had 700 locomotives, 25 per cent of the pre-war standard.'

When I asked about the status of King Leopold, he looked at me as if I had asked him to which political party did he belong. 'It seems to me that since the liberation of Belgium,

King Leopold has lost, and is still losing, popularity,' I continued

'King Leopold's position is certainly a difficult one,' he replied with a cynical smile.

'As a Belgian, the only thing I can say is that I think the present Regent has done a great job these past two years.'

After my co-traveller left the train, I reflected on the situation that King Leopold had found himself in. I had to remember that Germany held 70,000 Belgian prisoners of war, and later 600,000 Belgians were compelled to work for Germany. One false move by the King might have cost hundreds, if not thousands of lives.

I switched off the light in my compartment for a few hours' sleep. I wanted to be fully prepared for when the train rolled into Germany.

It wasn't fully daylight as the train crossed the frontier from Belgium into Germany. The last time I had turned my back on these borders, a grey-bearded German policeman wearing a swastika had said in a friendly, but firm voice, 'Take my advice. Never set foot on German soil again.'

Seven years had passed and the history of the world had undergone one of its most brutal and barbaric episodes ever.

Strategically, the Third Reich had disappeared from the geographical map of Europe, and from a military point of view democracy – with its principles of liberty and freedom – had achieved a complete victory over tyranny, oppression and persecution.

As a representative of those victorious principles, and as someone who served in the fight against the Nazi terror, I thought perhaps I should be proud to have made it back. I had defied the police warning, and here I was back to see the ruins of the 'Thousand Year Reich'.

But I had no feelings of hatred or revenge against a nation and its people who once put me in concentration camps, sent my mother to a death camp and forced me to leave. Military

118

victory was one thing, but I was not so convinced that the theoretical principles of freedom, for which millions of soldiers gave their lives, had come into practice. The German people were broken and the country was in a vulnerable position as the rest of Europe strived for world peace. People were starving.

I had a good idea of what the British public's opinion was of the German people, but I wanted to know about German attitudes towards their new situation. Had the German people still a destructive mind, or were they looking to be more constructive? If the psychological roots of Nazism had been destroyed, what had it been replaced with?

The rubble, the bricks and the vast empty hole that was once the Siegfried Line bore witness to the destructive process of the Allied bombardment, and that in itself seemed to make real daylight impossible on German soil.

Leaving the ruins of Aachen and Cologne, the train moved towards Osnabruck. Here I changed to a train that would take me directly to Berlin. I boarded a compartment for Allied personnel only, so I was quite surprised to see two Germans sitting in it. Later I learnt that they'd got special permission from the Allied authorities. They were lucky because these designated carriages were warm. The rest didn't even have any windows.

As we moved further into Germany the day got lighter and I got to see my first impression of Germans as they waited on various platforms. It wasn't pleasant.

You could tell the undernourishment from their faces. Some men still wore their army uniforms as they didn't have other clothes, and the women looked shabby.

At Dortmund station a boy ran up and down the platform selling copies of the *New York Herald* and *Daily Mail*. When he saw me in a comfortable carriage standing at the window for a cigarette with a few British Officers and a Frenchman, he looked disgusted. In a very fast Westphalian dialect he said to his fellow countrymen, 'Look at these men! Germany will only be ours when we are able to use our own trains again.'

When the boy saw me smile, he knew I had understood what he said and quickly disappeared into the crowd. Nothing could have better expressed the true German feeling than the remarks of this young paperboy.

Soon I realised now that the former master race had transformed itself into a slave nation. Suddenly the Germans were terribly polite. They were helpful and treated every foreigner like a superbeing. Perhaps they had expected that this is how we would have been if the Führer had set foot on English or American soil.

Personally I didn't feel these Germans knew the real meaning of democracy, and I was sorry to see that the occupation army didn't act very democratically either. They were more like individual dictators.

When the train arrived at Hanover, the cold German compartments became overcrowded. As there was plenty of room in ours, a German policeman politely asked if we would mind if an elderly German lady could take a seat. None of us objected, but soon after she took her seat an official from the train company opened the door demanding to know who had given her permission. 'Don't you know it's strictly forbidden for Germans to sit in here?' he yelled.

'These gentlemen were kind enough not to raise any objection,' she told him, to which the official retorted, 'There is a French lady standing in the corridor and she has the privilege of sitting in here so you must get out.'

But there was enough room for both women, so when the French lady arrived the elderly woman asked again if she could stay. This time she asked the lady.

'Certainly not,' she said, and the whole matter was settled.

This little incident reminded me of how the Nazis used to treat the Jews. There was no sign of democracy, humanity or any of the ideals here for which the Second World War was fought.

On the first day in Berlin I went for a walk through the cold and icy streets of the former capital of the Third Reich. The so-called 'West End' of the city, where I lived for years and used to know inside out, was hardly recognisable. Only the street names reminded me of places where former school pals used to live, and the house where I used to live was totally destroyed in a bombing raid.

There were only two big working class suburbs that were largely spared by the Allied bombardment. In the centre at the former Postdamer Platz and the Leipziger Strasse, there was not one house standing fit for a human to live in. Three quarters of the population of Berlin were now living in camps or shelters.

I saw ten people living in one cellar cleared of bomb debris, all trying to live on one weekly bread ration, but the availability of food in the city varied. The Russian sector had the most food, followed by the British and the French.

Whenever you had a conversation with the Germans, they all warned you not to go to the Russian sector as they felt it was very dangerous. However I wanted to find out the truth so I decided to go there to do a report.

The truth I found out was that in the Russian sector you could go anywhere without getting stopped, and hardly saw any soldiers. If you did they were very polite, and when Russian soldiers went on public transport you hardly noticed them.

I felt the fear of the Russians was only partly justified. History later revealed exactly how bad they were directly after the end of the war, but it should be added that not everyone in the British or US forces who came here acted like gentlemen either. However Russians in particular hadn't forgotten the Nazi army's behaviour in the Soviet Union.

Back in central Berlin, the main street for shopping and

social gathering Kurfurstendamm had become a dead alley, and the trams passing down it had their shattered windows replaced with just pieces of cardboard. In the evenings there was no entertainment as the only thing on people's minds was how to overcome this cold winter. Great epidemics had been predicted over the coming weeks. To keep warm people were literally burning their furniture. Some even paid 100 marks for a lethal injection so they could die in peace.

I went to have a meeting with Stadtrat Fullsack who was in charge of food distribution at the Berlin council. He deplored the obstacles to the recovery of the city represented by the zonal system and the failure to establish a valid German currency.

'We do not want hand outs from England and America,' he said. 'We want to work to buy our own materials and become self-sufficient.'

His comments about the zonal system reminded me of another conversation I had with a German concerning the amounts of wreckage visible everywhere. From the ruins of buildings, cars, trams and trucks there were still individual parts that clearly remained intact. I asked why these parts weren't rescued and used for repair work. I was told this was a naïve question as it was not as easy as I may think.

'Firstly buildings and vehicles lie in different zones,' I am reminded. 'To remove either glass or any other useful structures you would have to obtain four different permits. One for the removal, a second for the transport, a third to register it to where it had gone, and a fourth for an approval for what it was being used for. So we just leave the wreckage where it is.'

Two days before I left Berlin I took a taxi to the US Press headquarters in Zehlendorf. I had decided to travel to Frankfurt and needed to make sure that my press credentials and other documents were in order.

The American sector of Berlin was by far the best area of the former capital city as there was hardly any war damage.

122

Until now I had hardly seen any GIs, but here they occupied flats originally built for SS leaders.

On guard outside the Press HQ was a GI in a dark uniform. When I asked him directions to the Press Office he responded 'Me don't know.'

'Don't you speak any English?' I asked. 'Aren't you an American?'

'Not yet, but I hope to be one very soon,' he told me in German. He explained that he had signed with the American forces in Berlin but had to serve for a certain period before they would grant him citizenship. I had no time to pursue this conversation, but it was the first time I had heard of Germans in the American army.

The train for Frankfurt left Wannsee station at 5.40 p.m. and on arriving early some very young GIs examined my papers. I was required to pay seven dollars and seventy-five cents in script money for the journey.

Ten minutes later when I tried to board the train, two US army police asked to see my papers again, and before I sat in the compartment they were examined once more by the US transport police (known as 'snowdrops').

These snowdrops were anything but polite. Although they could not have seen more than a year or so in service, they evidently thought of themselves as being extremely important. Later I learnt that 95 per cent of the American occupational forces had never seen active war service, and looking at their long revolvers and medals for marksmanship I wondered whether the US War Department had chosen the best ambassadors here for democracy.

When the train arrived in Frankfurt the following morning, the compartment door had hardly been opened properly before a crowd of Germans burst in, fighting their way through the Allied compartments grovelling for left-overs of anything from bread and apples to even chewing gum. Only the snowdrops prevented them from fighting each other.

I phoned the US Press Hotel for a car to fetch me and was told I'd have to take a bus. After 20 minutes a special one for Allied personnel arrived and was told, 'You can't get on – you're German!'

After I showed him my press card and spoke to him in English he said, 'Sorry, OK you are not German you can get on.'

By now I really had come to the conclusion that the amount of red tape I thought only possible in the British zone of Germany was actually exceeded in the US Zone.

When I said 'goodbye' again to the dust and rubble of Germany on my return to England my head was full of questions about how so many problems could be resolved. It occurred to me that the psychological roots of Nazism could not have found a better ground for rebirth than in a starving Germany. Was there the danger of a new Hitler, or had the German people learned the consequences of such a tragedy? I honestly didn't know.

Chapter Ten

After arriving back in London I wrote about my recent journey and returned to work at Joe Lyons. The trip had made a big impression on me and I was determined to do it again as soon as possible.

Fortunately *Peace News* was very pleased with my report and in March 1948 sent me again to Berlin, this time as correspondent for *United Nations News* too.

Three years after the war the situation here was still serious, and it had taken until now for the Allied Forces to realise that whatever system might be put back in place for Germany, it would always be the capital of the German Reich.

Despite the ruins clearly visible from my window at the Hotel Am Zoo, Berlin still had a life of its own and was slowly recovering. Still the Germans were unsure what the Russians and Americans would do, and some Berliners continued to queue at post offices to send possessions into safety.

I went to visit my uncle, brother of my foster mother, and a survivor of the Third Reich who now worked in the building trade. He told me that all my Jewish relatives had been sent to concentration camps and not returned. One cousin had tried to escape the Gestapo by jumping out of a window and broke his legs. The Gestapo had first sent him to hospital, but as soon as he could walk again he was sent to the gas chamber.

Berlin had become a chief fortress in the Cold War. The Western Sectors had become isolated, and when I tried to enter the Russian sector this time, my German driver looked nervous and told me that one of his colleagues had disappeared there.

When he went looking for him, the Russians put him in a cellar and would only release him if he signed a document declaring he was a British spy sent by MI5 in London.

Later the Russian-sponsored German press reported that British journalists were spying so gave Russian authorities stronger measures against foreigners entering their sector.

In view of this, it was surprising the American, British and French authorities did not collaborate in resisting the pressure from the East.

However it would be an exaggeration to say that a panic had broken out in the city, even though this had been reported by some of my colleagues in the press.

Even though the atmosphere here was still nerve-racking, I could also see from my hotel a peaceful population queuing for the cinema and enjoying a quiet life.

Before leaving Berlin I witnessed the East German government close the border from Berlin into West Germany and for the first time I had to board an aeroplane to depart the city. It took me to Hamburg where I took a plane back to London.

Back washing dishes, I was delighted to hear from Professor Jourdan again who told me I wouldn't have to work at Joe Lyons for much longer. He was to become Director of the French Institute in South Kensington and would give me a job.

Keeping to his word, he gave me a small office in the scientific section of the Institute's library run by a Madame Chauvy, and gave me the post of librarian. I was paid the princely sum of £5 a week and was also allowed to do freelance writing in open hours as well in my spare time.

Since I had seen the Professor in Berlin he had got married to a pretty French girl Denise, who spoke very little English.

Although my French was restricted to what I learnt at school and my six months with the BEF in 1940, I acted as her interpreter when she did her weekly shopping at a market in Kings Cross.

To be such a good friend of the Director also allowed me to attend many important events and gatherings at the Institute. I was there when the Queen Mother and new French President Vincent Auriol visited, and was introduced to the Duchess of Kent and Baroness Butberg (once wife of the author Maxim Gorki).

I offered her my article 'The SS – The Last Defender Of Nazism' which had already been published in the prestigious *Army Quarterly*. She accepted the piece on behalf of *La France Libre* and it was soon translated into French and published.

Then, on July 8, 1948 I got married. The Professor was my Best Man, and my wife Joan and I enjoyed a fortnight in Jersey after a small civil wedding.

We began married life with a small, furnished room in Earls Court. Joan worked at the Town Hall in Edgware Road, while I carried on at the Institute in the library while furthering my career in journalism.

That was until after almost two years when I became aware that certain other members of staff had become jealous of my position and close friendship with the Professor. I thought it only fair that I should leave and carry on with my journalism independently.

As it turned out, it was a good time to do this because in post-war Germany and Austria, many publications were looking for new writers. Many of the editors were survivors of the war who had been opposed to the Third Reich.

In August 1949 I returned to Germany, not as an official accredited journalist this time, but as a tourist with my wife.

We took a flight from Northolt, a commercial airport then (before becoming the RAF base it is now), and landed in

Düsseldorf. On the journey from the aerodrome to the centre the sights we saw were like a nightmare in the middle of the day.

My wife kept asking, 'How is it possible for the people of Düsseldorf to live in these ruins?'

We saw people coming out of holes in building remains that looked as if they were going to collapse at any minute. Nowhere in German had I seen destruction as extreme as here, and you couldn't help feel sorry for the plight, which the Germans had brought upon themselves.

However these feelings of pity changed when we arrived in the centre town of Ruhr. Here the café houses were overcrowded with customers enjoying ice cream and pastries and the central shopping streets were already trading quality goods. It seemed unbelievable that such life could exist among the ruins. Despite the destruction, which I called 'The death of a nation', the Germans were on the up again and were fast trying to forget the recent past.

I was told that despite how it looked, Germany was still living on charity from America. However the middle class, who lost most of their savings during the war, were starting to put money back into the banks again and this was a good start for the country's own recovery. Also there had been a currency reform and the D-Mark was developing nicely into a forceful purchasing power.

Next my wife and I continued our journey down the Rhine to Cologne, and then Bonn. On the Sunday we made a trip on the Rhine towards Koblenz. The ship was packed with German holidaymakers and I think we were the only foreigners on it.

As the journey continued, many of the Germans became tipsy and started to sing and tell jokes so everyone could hear them. They began with German folk songs about wine and the Rhine, but then one party started singing, 'We are marching; We are marching against...' They didn't dare want to say England, but in laughing voices they continued 'Drachenfels...'

Everybody on the ship knew what they meant, and the applause that followed was like a political demonstration – right here in the British zone of Germany!

The ship bore the name of the Iron Chancellor Bismarck, and the Captain looked like a former U-Boat Commandant who had gone back to sea again – only this time as a ticket collector.

The political jokes that followed were not jokes at all, but one insult after another against Britain, France and America. It was then that I saw Germans exactly as they were 15 years ago when on the same trip you would see swastikas flying along the Rhine.

This time it wasn't the swastika, but the spirit of Potsdam, the Potsdam of 1933 where Hitler united the ideals with those of the aged German Field Marshal von Hindenburg.

We spent the evening after our boat trip at a German home. A lady who worked as a cleaner at the hotel where we were staying had invited us. Her daughter had married an English soldier and she was very anxious to give us hospitality in her well-furnished flat in Bonn.

We told her about our experiences on the ship and she nodded and said, 'That is nothing. Practically everyone here is a Nazi and we daren't say anything against them as they all have good positions and they could make life very difficult.

'Mind you,' she continued, 'it's the fault of the British, they are too easy going. Too good.'

Back in London there were tensions too, particularly with the housing problem as damaged homes were still common and clearly visible at this time.

The problem appeared to be production costs. A typical three-bedroom house was three and a quarter times more expensive to build in 1948 than it was just before the war, due mainly to the cost of raw materials and labour.

Elsewhere shops were full of goods, but people were short of money and placed what little they have on the Football Pools hoping for a big win.

My wife and I moved temporarily into my mother and father-in-law's home as a means of saving money, and soon I came to a decision. While I would continue to work as a freelance political journalist, I was going to broaden my area of writing into show business.

I'd been interested in films since my teenage years in Berlin, and there was now a post-war film industry starting to boom in Britain as well as America.

It was time to give it a try.

Chapter Eleven

By the late 1940s, British film companies were keen to get as much foreign press as they could to generate business in Europe, so I contacted some Austrian and German film magazines that were not represented in London.

Soon I was fortunate to have been appointed London correspondent for a film journal and went to introduce myself to the Associated Pictures Corporation and the J. Arthur Rank Organisation. But it wasn't long before I had my first confrontation with Rank.

It was after I had written a negative critique about a Margaret Lockwood film that appeared in a Düsseldorf daily paper.

Rank stopped sending me press tickets for their films and I reported this back to the Editor of my film journal in Germany.

'What happened to the freedom of the press?' they asked the Rank representative in Hamburg.

It was a difficult time for foreign journalists in London because the major film companies wanted support, but also did not want too much coverage of their films abroad until closer to their release date. This would often be a good year after British audiences had seen it.

At the same time there were German and Austrian stars looking to make their mark with British audiences.

When a film was being made at a British studio the press were often invited to meet the stars on set and on one of my first assignments I met Noel Coward. He was at Pinewood

Studios making *The Astonished Heart* (1949) with Celia Johnson.

I stood and watched one of the scenes being filmed and was then introduced to one of the biggest names in film, music and theatre in the 20th century.

'I am very pleased to meet you,' said Mr Coward in broken German, adding, 'Mein Deutsch ist nicht sehr gut.' (My German isn't good!)

'We can talk in English,' I replied

'Oh das ist fabelhaft!' smiled Mr Coward before I asked him if he was planning to make any more films in Germany or Austria.

'Yes I would like that,' he said, 'But I haven't got the time.'

I asked him whether he had been back to Germany at all since the end of the war.

'I'm afraid not, but I still have fond memories of the many friends I made there.'

Another of the first actors I met was Douglas Fairbanks Jnr at Shepperton Studios while filming *State Secret* (1950). The American star had also acted as a special envoy for American President Roosevelt in Brazil, Argentina, Panama and Peru, and after the end of the war took an active part in supporting the Care Organisation to help Germany and Austria.

When I asked him what he thought about the Cold War which had just started he replied, 'You as a journalist can answer that question. I am now an actor, not a politician.'

Knowing that he had made films with Greta Garbo, Gertrude Lawrence, Elisabeth Bergner, Katherine Hepburn and Joan Crawford, I asked him who was the most beautiful actress he had played alongside.

He smiled. 'Sure you don't expect me to answer that. All my leading ladies were not only very beautiful women, but also great actresses.'

All film companies threw cocktail parties after the press

shows in the '50s, and this was where journalists were often able to meet their stars.

In 1951 the Savoy Hotel played host to Ava Gardner and I met her briefly to ask how she had enjoyed Berlin on a recent visit. 'It was very nice,' she told me, relieved that I hadn't mentioned her on/off relation with Frank Sinatra or that the talk of the party was that she was having an affair with Spanish bullfighter Mario Cabre, one of the co-stars in the film *Pandora & The Flying Dutchman* she was here to promote.

Later I met Marlene Dietrich, the daughter of a Prussian Officer, who had become a very successful star and who was in London to film *No Highway* (1951) with James Stewart. She was also from Berlin so I was keen to meet her.

After the reception at the Dorchester Hotel I took the liberty of sending her a song composed by my brother-in-law, Robb Morrison, but it was sent back with a letter, 'Thank you for sending me this. I thought I'd better send it back so that it doesn't get lost. I don't need any songs at this time. Many thanks again, Marlene.'

This handwritten note is one of my show business souvenirs.

Long before Elizabeth Taylor became talk of the town with her love affairs, I met her at one such party in London promoting her film *Ivanhoe* (1952).

She was here while on her honeymoon with first husband Nick Hilton, who accompanied her and showed some interest in a German women's journal I showed him.

No one at the time would have thought that this very pretty actress from Hampstead would survive six marriages and still make the cover headlines in newspapers in the year 2000.

Another party I attended was for the launch of the film *Oh ... Rosalinda* in 1955. It starred Mel Ferrer, once the husband of Audrey Hepburn, with Anneliese Rothenberger in the leading role along with Austrian actor Oskar Sima.

133

The Austrian star arrived nearly two hours late, so I asked him why.

'Well I just arrived by train from Vienna,' he said, knowing that the film company had paid for his air ticket. The star certainly wasn't short of money, yet he pocketed the fee for the air ticket.

'I saved the money,' he said, thinking perhaps this would make a good story in the Austrian press. But he was disappointed as only a very few journalists took any notice of this behaviour.

Also in the film was Austrian actor Anton Walbrook (a descendant of a family of circus clowns), but I didn't meet him at the launch, I was invited round to have tea with him instead at his Hampstead home. He told me that the Nazi Propaganda Minister, Goebbels, had tried to persuade him to stay in Germany despite the fact that his grandmother was Jewish.

'Goebbels wanted to make me an "Ehren Arier" (an honorable non-Jewish citizen),' said Walbrook, 'but I refused to stay there and went to the USA. However at first some people there refused to be associated with me as they thought I had some sympathy with Nazi Germany.

'In 1937 I had my first success in Britain with *Victoria The Great* and have been here since.' Naturally I asked if he would ever go back to Germany.

'No, never!' he insisted, but a few years later when the German D-Mark became hard currency he was back at Geiselgasteig, the film studios outside Munich. Also, in 1961 he played Johann Strauss in *Vienna Waltzes*, shot in Vienna itself where he had been born in 1900.

By the time Hildegard Knef came to London with the film *Svengali* in 1954, she was already a famous film star in Germany. She was keen to make an impression on British audiences but I was dumbfounded when her PR lady Elly Silman told me that Frau Knef did not want to see anyone from the German press.

However, when my story was published back in Germany with a heading 'Hildegard Knef Antwortet Nicht' ('Hildegard Knef Doesn't Respond'), Elly Silman was back on the phone within 48 hours to protest and grant an immediate interview.

I took along Stephan Glass, a well-known photographer who had emigrated from Berlin after Hitler came to power (his brother Zoltan Glass, incidentally was an official photographer at the wedding of Grace Kelly to Prince Rainier), and it all went very well.

The first time I'd seen Hildegard was at the London premier of *The Sinner* (1950), just after it had been translated into English. I was attending as representative of *Film Echo*, and afterwards at the reception I met Henri Nannen, Editor-in-Chief of the German magazine *Stern*.

At one point during the evening Henri took me to one side and asked me not to mention in my report that he'd met me in London with Miss Knef. Who was he trying to keep this 'excursion' from?

I had also met Henri Nannen before. I had been appointed London correspondent of the *Grosse Oesterreich Illustrierte* and the Editor-in-Chief, Mr Sawalish, suggested I meet him while he stayed at the Half Moon Hotel near Piccadilly Circus.

The idea was that Mr Nannen might be interested in a freelance contributor such as myself. When I entered the breakfast room at the hotel, Herr Nannen immediately complained about the service. He had ordered breakfast in a loud voice at 9.00 a.m. and was still waiting at 9.30.

What had happened was that the waitress, who had taken the order, wasn't very pleased with her arrogant German customer, so as she was going off duty after nine she didn't pass on the order to her successor.

This certainly caused some trouble, and I could tell that my own presence wasn't welcome and wasn't going to lead anywhere. Herr Nannen had already a permanent London correspondent.

The next time I met the Editor-in-Chief of *Stern* was in Hamburg after my pictures were ready. Assuming he had a special friendship with Miss Knef I took them directly to his office. I also told him Frau Knef had just arrived in Hamburg to stay at the Atlantic Hotel, but he didn't believe me.

Before looking at my pictures he had his secretary phone the hotel that confirmed the guest was in residence.

Henri Nannen chose five of my pictures and without any hesitation agreed a payment of DM300. I didn't even have to wait for the money. He gave me a play slip that I could cash before even leaving the building.

This was my last meeting with the Newspaper King of Hamburg, who successfully made *Stern* the number one weekly illustrated magazine in Germany from 1955 to 1990.

Before I left Hamburg I received a call from George Top who worked for the Decca record company in Germany. He explained the 'forces sweetheart' Vera Lynn was arriving to record some music and he'd been told to meet her at the railway station.

The problem was that he didn't speak any English so I was asked whether I could meet her and her husband Harry Lewis and escort them to the hotel.

When they arrived they asked me if I would mind taking them sightseeing so we took a taxi for a drive around and Vera told me that now she was known in England, the USA, Holland, Denmark and France, she would liked to become well-known in Germany.

Decca in Germany were planning to release 'Auf Wiedersehn Sweetheart' that was a No. 1 hit in the USA having just had her first No. 1 hit in Britain with 'My Son, My Son'. (There were only pop charts in Britain since 1952, so it wouldn't have been possible to have a No. 1 in 1942 with 'We'll Meet Again'.)

In 1957 I went to a cocktail party given by the film

producer Ivan Foxwell after the press show of the film *Manuela* starring Trevor Howard and Elsa Martinelli.

I had met Trevor Howard when he played opposite the French star Anouk Aimée in *Golden Salamander* (1950), the first British part for the unknown young French actress after the war.

It wasn't a special cocktail party, the same crowd of critics present, and if you didn't remember their name you knew their faces.

During a drink at the Hungarian restaurant in Dean Street, which was always popular, I met the film critic from the *Daily Express*, Leonard Mosley. He told me he was writing a book about a real life double agent during the Second World War.

He thought the spy was still alive somewhere in Europe but didn't know where. When he found out I had good contacts in Germany he thought that perhaps I could find the man who betrayed Rommel and Montgomery's secrets.

Leonard knew that I had interviewed the owner of the Dreesen Hotel in Bad Godesberg shortly after the war, who assured me that he was never a Nazi. It was from this same hotel near Bonn that Neville Chamberlain returned from a meeting with Hitler in 1938 waving the note, 'Peace in our time'.

Leonard asked me if I would look for the spy in Germany. He was lucky as I was preparing a short trip to Hamburg to see editors again, and then off to Düsseldorf, Nuremberg and Munich.

In Hamburg I met an old girlfriend of mine, who was married to one of the top German photographers and secretary to one of the directors of the publishing group, Axel Springer.

We had known each other before the war and when I asked her about my search for the double agent she said, 'You may be lucky, there is a series of articles published in the weekly journal *Kristall* about the Africa Corps written

137

by Paul Carrell. I am sure this is a pen name of a former member of the Nazi party.'

In less than 48 hours I got the address of Paul Carrell, whose real name was Paul Schmidt, the interpreter for the Nazi Foreign Minister Joachim von Ribbentrop and Hitler. He lived in the Ise Strasse on the fifth floor where I visited him.

There are sometimes situations in life that you cannot explain, such as when you shake hands with a stranger and know immediately that you can get on with him. When I met Ribbentrop's press chief I knew he had taken a liking to me and the feeling was mutual.

I told him that I was a survivor of the concentration camps of Dachau and Buchenwald and for a second he looked at me slightly shocked. Then he said, 'Certainly I'll help you. The man you are looking for isn't in Hamburg, as he is working for the Deuxième Bureau in Strasburg. When do you want to meet him?'

'Well it isn't me who wants to meet him, it is a very good friend of mine in London who is writing a book about Rommel and Monty and he is looking for him as he is the key figure in his book. My friend represents the *Daily Express* as a film critic.'

'You being a former concentration camp prisoner, I'll help you,' said Herr Schmidt. I really knew that by helping me he was trying to whitewash his guilty conscience of the past.

I flew back to London with the information and made another appointment to visit Herr Schmidt with Leonard Mosley in the presence of the famous double agent.

He called himself John Eppler, but was actually an Egyptian named Hussein Gaafer, and when we met up, Leonard was very nervous and did not expect the friendliness of the German spy and ex-Nazi who had masqueraded as an Arabic interpreter. When his story was serialised in the *Sunday*

Express, he said that he'd put a pistol on the table to make Eppler talk.

But there was no pistol only a cup of coffee! And after the interview Leonard wrote the story in his hotel room through the night and until daylight with a bottle of whisky next to his typewriter.

I mention this for those interested in historical fact rather than fiction. Leonard's book on the episode was also made into a film *Foxhole In Cairo* starring Michael Caine (1960).

Albert Lieven played the German General in the film. He was another Berliner who fled Germany in the 1930s and often played military roles in films. When I met him at Pinewood studios I asked (in German) whether he had any intentions of returning to Germany.

'No, not really' he replied (in English), saying that having left Germany 16 years ago he could hardly even remember the language.

He told me his father wanted him to study Biology in Berlin, but during the financial crisis his father lost a fortune and Albert was forced to take a clerical bank job.

'During my free time I visited the theatre and the opera, and when Hitler came to power I realised I wouldn't have a chance to fulfill my ambition to become an actor.'

When he was later asked to speak German in an English film he had to practise his own mother tongue.

Meanwhile, during one of my weekly visits to the different film journals in Fleet Street I met the Editor-in-Chief of the weekly publication *Picture Show*. Her name was Mrs Edith Napier and she was a former Rumanian Princess.

I asked her if the journal was represented on the forthcoming Berlin Film Festival (1957). 'No I am not represented. If you want to go you can represent us,' she told me.

So I wrote to the Director of the Film Festival, Herr Bauer, and received my invitation.

Britain's contribution was the ABC production *Woman in*

139

a *Dressing Gown*, a film directed and co-produced by J. Lee Thompson with a script by Ted Willis.

The film's Chief Producer was Frank Godwin who I met later in London (1959) while at lunch in Isows with Philip Jacob of the Anglo Amalgamated Film Company.

Isows was a Jewish restaurant in Soho and a favourite meeting place for well-known personalities. Some, like Diana Dors, Cliff Richard and Nat Cohen, even had their names engraved on their own special seats.

On this occasion I was introduced to Frank, who asked me if I could recommend a good-looking German starlet for a leading role in a production he was working on. By chance I happened to have a copy of the German magazine *Gondel* with me with pictures of pin-up Elke Sommer.

'You know this girl?' he asked. I told him I had never met her, but I knew she spoke good English because she had been an au pair in England for a couple of years. I also knew she was now living in Nuremberg and could be contacted via Arthur Brauner, the German film producer.

Frank thanked me, and three months later sent me an invitation to the Dorchester Hotel for a special cocktail party – to meet Elke Sommer and Richard Todd at the launch of her first British film *Don't Bother To Knock* (1960).

Back to my trip to the Berlin Film Festival, I reacquainted myself with Ted Willis who I'd previously met when he was Editor-in-Chief of the left-wing journal *Challenge*. He had published some of my contributions (he later became Lord Willis).

He was excited about the success of *Woman In A Dressing Gown* which won a special prize, the 'Berlin Golden Baer' at the festival.

Sylvia Sims, Anthony Quayle and Yvonne Mitchell played lead roles, and I was introduced to the film's Press Officer, Bob Webb.

He told me he was having to deal with the diva like

behavior of Yvonne Mitchell who refused to fly to Berlin, insisted on coming by train and demanded a special apartment either on the ground floor or first floor of her hotel. Perhaps mild by today's standards.

Yvonne also starred in 1959's *Tiger Bay* alongside John Mills who I'd met earlier in the year while shooting this film that featured the first leading role by his daughter Hayley Mills.

Famous Hollywood stars and not so famous British stars were in attendance here. One of the not so well-known ones was Mara Lane who I had first met in London. I had visited her flat at Hyde Park Corner where she lived with her mother Mrs Bolton and sister Jackie (who also had a few small parts in British films before marrying a Spanish Prince).

I had interviewed Mara for a German monthly because she was originally from Vienna and had been making films consistently since *Affair In Monte Carlo* in 1953.

She'd been invited to the Festival as a guest of John Wolf, boss of Romulus Films, but despite having a new film *Love From Paris* in 1957, they didn't show any of her work.

The British Press was well represented here, as usual, and I met one its characters, Mr Silvermann from the *British Provincial* newspaper. It was a well-known joke that Silverman rented a furnished room outside a public telephone box and gave his contact number as the box with a note of what time he could accept calls.

He even left the windows of his room open so he could hear the ringing!

Twenty-five years later he died in a rest home in Hampstead shortly after he had celebrated his 94th birthday.

There was definitely no shortage of entertainment around Berlin while I was there for the festival, and it was good to see the city was slowly recovering from the destruction of the Second World War.

Back in England one of the best opportunities I had in

141

1958 for an interview and some pictures was with Ingrid Bergman. She was shooting *Indiscreet* at Elstree Studios, but as usual we were only allocated a brief time between takes and on the day this was shorter than usual. She told me she was looking forward to going to Hong Kong as soon as she finished filming, but that was as much as I got from this film legend on the day.

One if the biggest stars I met as a film journalist was undoubtedly Maurice Chavalier, the most famous French star of the 1930s and '40s, who in *Gigi* sang his classic song 'Thank Heaven for Little Girls'. In fact I interviewed him twice, although the first time he objected to my line of questioning.

When we first met it was at the studios of the BBC where he was preparing for a programme *Café Continental* that was about to be broadcasted. The next time it was at Pinewood Studios when he had the leading role in the 1960 Walt Disney film *In Search of the Castaways*.

'We meet again, Mr Chevalier!' I said to the star, who looked shocked to see me. I suspected he remembered my first ever question to him at our last meeting which was, 'Why did you collaborate with the Germans during the occupation of your country?'

He was absolutely furious. 'No, I did not collaborate with the Nazis, I was forced to sing and I was hoping to help the French prisoners of war.'

'You knew the Nazis better than I did, having been in a concentration camp, and knew that I had no chance of refusing an order from the Nazi High Command,' he said standing next to me smelling of garlic. We cleared the air on this second meeting.

Maurice wasn't the only well-known person to know of my prison past under the Nazis on this day with the French star at Pinewood – so did Walt Disney himself, at least he did by the end of our meeting.

142

Because of my background I was often asked about my pre-war days in Berlin and life in England. Sometimes they asked me more questions than I could ask myself in an interview and this was definitely the case with Walt Disney.

He was fascinated with my past, which made it difficult to get the answers I needed in the short time I was allocated to meet this cartoon and film legend. Still he was very friendly and had no objection to being photographed – unlike so many other stars I met over the years.

Gert Froebe, however, was definitely not shy of the camera although he was nervous of television. When I met the star of *The Longest Day*, *Those Magnificent Men In Their Flying Machines*, and the James Bond film *Goldfinger*, he said, 'I feel that if people could see me on television, they wouldn't come to see me at the cinema.'

When we met in Ireland, he was filming *Rocket To The Moon* (1967) with Dennis Price. 'I also believe showing films on television was a bad move,' he added. 'It could hurt the film industry.'

In 1966 I met Sophia Loren who was filming *Arabesque* at Pinewood Studios. She was definitely not shy and in her younger years had been a pin-up girl in magazines. I asked her whether these had been of help in her career.

'Definitely not!' she said, 'And I would like to give some advice to young actresses – pin-up pictures are not always an asset in your career.'

I reminded her that Marilyn Monroe had become well known and popular through her pin-up pictures.

Sophia thought for a second and the said, 'Well you shouldn't forget that most of Marilyn's films had parts in them which often lent themselves to being sexy pin-up pictures afterwards.'

I asked her if she would like to play Eva Peron in a film version being prepared. She replied that she had read the script and turned it down.

143

'Are you opposed to films which have a political background, perhaps because your sister is married to a son of Mussolini?' I asked.

Sophia smiled. 'No I don't have such a prejudice. In fact I've just finished a film about the development of the V2 rocket. It's more important that a film script should have artistic qualities. I am an independent actress and I can choose any roles I want to play.'

At this time Sophia hadn't yet married Carlo Ponti, but it was well known that they were very close and it was obvious to ask about a possible wedding. It was also reported in the press that Carlo's divorce from his Italian wife had hit legal difficulties. Sophia Loren told me that she would never give up Carlo, and sure enough by the next time I met her they were married.

Meeting her again when she filmed the lead role in *A Countess From Hong Kong* (1967), directed by Charlie Chaplin, was more difficult.

We also had to agree not to take any photographs during the shooting of the film, and any taken afterwards had to be shown to Sophia before publication.

However, once on the film set my photographer disobeyed the rules and without my knowledge took some unauthorised pictures. When this came out we were both banned from the studio until further notice and the magazine I represented tried to pacify her with great coverage of the film and a huge bunch of red roses delivered before the premiere.

Another of my more difficult episodes was meeting Eartha Kitt who was in London to promote *Saint of Devil's Island* (1961). Orson Wells once described her as 'the most exciting woman ever born', but when I asked her whether she happened to speak a little German she said, 'What do you think I am, a linguist? Why does everybody ask me such stupid questions?!'

After this she stormed off in a temper leaving the Press

144

Officer of the film to tell me I'd been unlucky and that I should wait for her to calm down. A few minutes she came back and said, 'I'm sorry if I sounded offensive.' She explained Spanish, French and Italian journalists had just asked her whether she could speak their languages.

(Eartha also met my son Ralph who she hit with a plastic flower when he interviewed her for a music magazine in the 1980s.)

One of my most interesting friends from the world of show business world was Doctor Max Odens, a 'doctor to the stars' with a practice in Harley Street.

Both he and his wife Hanny were from Berlin, in fact Hanny survived the concentration camp of Ravensbruck, and had lived in the same street in Berlin as me during the first 19 years of my life. Hanny and I were also good friends but she never liked to talk about the concentration camp years.

Max left Berlin in the 1930s and worked for the Red Cross during the Second World War. Afterwards he became a successful doctor and gynaecologist with many impressive clients including the Prime Minister of India Mrs Indira Gandhi.

We met through a mutual friend and publicist Cathy O'Brian who looked after a lot of Hollywood stars when they came to Britain, and if anyone became ill or needed a doctor, she would send them to see Max. When Hildegard Knef expected her first baby, she consulted him during her stay in London.

Max was a character with plenty of jokes and always craved attention and publicity. We saw each other a lot through similar contacts in the press world, and in 1958 he threw me a lavish 40th birthday party at The Caprice. He also assisted my wife and me adopting Ralph (1960) and Helen (1963), becoming their godfather.

He was a great supporter of the Swiss surgeon Professor Paul Niehans, famous for his research into prolonging life. The Professor used to prescribe his own special life-extending pill to his patients that at that time was only obtainable in Germany and Switzerland. Max was very keen to get some and on my next trip to Zurich sent me to get him a box for his famous clients.

In the meantime through his own research he managed to extend the life of a group of rats by three times their normal span, an experiment that in medical history books was the first and only of its kind!

In November 1963, Max and Hanny threw a Friday night party to warm their new home in Dunrobin Court, off the Finchley Road. My wife Joan and I left Ralph and baby Helen with Joan's parents for the occasion, and we went to the party where Max had also invited the famous bandleader Jack Hylton.

I enjoyed meeting Jack because I remembered going to see him perform in Berlin during the 1930s. He also helped me set up an interview with Shirley Bassey when she played at the Adelphi. Jack was accompanied by his latest lady friend, Miss Australia, who I had met before at Elstree Studios when she had a part in the film *Girl At Arms*.

Also there was the owner of the Sunday Newspaper *News Of The World*, and the well-known publicist Bill Bachelor who represented Otto Preminger's film *Joan of Arc*, and our friend Cathy O'Brian who was representing Robert Mitchum when he filmed in Elstree.

The well-known journalist Mr Pem and his wife were there too. Pem, who was once the London correspondent of *Hollywood Reporter*, now had his own weekly newsheet *Pem's Newsletter* with a circulation of over 100 copies for subscribers only. The *Newsletter* was more or less a who's who in show business, and Max was always anxious to get a mention.

All the personalities Pem had mentioned in his publication where more or less well known in the 20th century. He had met Billy Wilder who had started the Austrian daily paper

Wiener Montag before the Second World War and who I had been told about in the concentration camp, Dachau.

My fellow prisoner Maximilian Reich had once told me that if I ever would see freedom again, I should contact Billy Wilder because he would be of great assistance. Unfortunately I never had the opportunity.

Going back to Max's party, his wife Hanny (who contrary to her husband wasn't a great friend of publicity) was a very good hostess and the party should have been a very joyful occasion.

However at about 9.00 p.m. the phone rang and Max came over to me to say the call was for me.

'Hello Gerd,' said the voice on the other side of the phone, 'I am Brian Clifford, the Picture Editor of the *Daily Herald.* I have an exclusive story for you.'

Brian knew that at this time I was representing several German weekly publications.

'I have had a wire report from the USA saying that President Kennedy has been assassinated.' The news this Friday November 22 was certainly a shock, and when I returned to the party with the news, Max quickly brought the evening to an end.

Max had a lot in common with the stars I met and interviewed in that they were all publicity seekers. In fact Max once got upset with me because I was listed in the prestigious *Who's Who?* international personality directory one year, something he had never achieved.

While stars liked to impress journalists, their PR agents often saw the other side of these people when they weren't getting the attention they felt they deserved.

The PR agent to English star Michael Rennie once told me that his client, who had starred in *The Third Man* and *The Lost World* among others, complained that he wasn't getting enough publicity. So he said, 'I can get you the headline in all the papers if you hang yourself.' They didn't speak after that.

147

Publicity was important to all the stars. The famous film producer Otto Preminger once told me, 'I would rather have bad publicity than no publicity at all.'

He was not the first (or last) to say this, but his turn was when we met at a press reception for the film *Saint Joan* (1957). While we were there he noticed that the critic from the *Daily Mirror* was missing and asked the PR agent where he was. The response was the agent didn't like the writer, to which Otto erupted, 'For my money you don't like him?' He was furious and hired a brand new agent Bill Batchelor.

Before we left the party Otto told me that if I ever wrote my memoirs he would like the film rights. Sadly he died in 1986.

Chapter Twelve

In 1959, while still in Wardour Street covering the films being made in Elstree, Pinewood and Shepperton, I returned to Fleet Street for a new job working for the German publication *Bunte Illustrierte*.

The owner was Dr Franz Burda who, I discovered was looking for a London representative. He was in London so I contacted him and we met.

One of the first things he asked me was, 'Are you clever?' I was a bit taken aback by this and assumed that what he really meant by this was 'am I well connected?'.

I told him that I had over the years built up some excellent connections in Fleet Street. I also explained that I was preparing to go to Germany and suggested I could call in at his head office in Offenburg.

So that's how it started, and about four weeks later we met again in Germany and this time I was offered a job for a monthly retainer of DM 750.

While in Germany I went to Munich, a place I well remembered because of the time I spent in a police cell there, surrounded by criminals, political prisoners, homosexuals and foreigners awaiting to be deported back to their own country.

Now 25 years later, I had not only survived a concentration camp, but also had managed to become a well-known foreign correspondent for a number of leading magazines and journals.

I decided to visit Dachau again, and when I told the young taxi driver my destination his eyes went wide with amazement.

149

'Why on earth do you want to go there?' he asked. 'It's the blackest spot in German history.'

'I was once a prisoner there,' I replied and his eyes opened even wider. He looked too young to have been a soldier during the war years, and after a while he said, 'Sir, forgive me, but we are not all criminals in Germany. We're not all ex-Nazis you know, and those that were must have been hypnotised by the devil.'

About 40 minutes later we drove down Dachauer Strasse and arrived at the gate of the concentration camp.

Dachau had certainly been transformed. The hut I was once billeted in and all but one like it had disappeared, and one large stone (like a gravestone) stood where they all once where. The one hut left was now a museum giving visitors the history in text and pictures of starved inmates before the liberation by the Americans in 1945.

The elderly tour guide asked me why I was so interested in wanting to see the camp, and I explained that I had been a prisoner in Hut 4 and Hut 6 back in 1938.

To my astonishment he replied, 'Why, I was a prisoner then too! It seems that because political prisoners and Jewish prisoners were in different huts, we never met or saw each other.'

I asked him why on earth he wanted to be a camp guide when it could only be a place filled with terrible memories.

'People should know what it was like under the Third Reich,' he said, 'And who better to tell them all about it than me? Besides, my dear friend, I am an old man, I suffer from TB and my pension isn't enough. I need the money.'

Back in London I received a special request from *Bunte* to help cover the story of a murder case in South Tyrol.

A reporter was sent to contact me as the murderer was supposed to have escaped to London. I told the reporter that I had not heard of the case, so he asked me where I thought a stranger in London would go if he only had little knowledge of the English language.

I suggested that he should visit Soho where German, Austrian and Swiss restaurants are situated.

Two days after my meeting with the reporter he called me again and told me thanks to my information he had traced the person who had committed the murder.

Two years later that reporter, whose name was Wolfgang Willman, was appointed Editor-in-Chief of one of Bauer's weekly publications called *Praline*.

When I visited Hamburg again I called in to see him, and he asked if I would like to become the London correspondent of *Praline* which I accepted. I never signed an exclusive contract with any German or Austrian publisher. I was in a position to represent several German and Austrian publications at the same time.

Certainly representing the Burda Publishing House from 1959 until 1966 was one of my most interesting periods as a journalist. 'Senator' Franz Burda was publisher of *Das Ufer* and *Bunte* when we met, but during my term as his London correspondent he had acquired the *Munchner Illustrierte*, *Stuttgart Illustrierte* and *Frankfurter Illustrierte*. 'Senator' Franz Burda became the uncrowned king in the German publishing world.

When the Queen and Prince Philip made their first state visit to Germany, the 'Senator' covered the Royal events and sent a special photographer.

Afterwards he phoned me in London and said 'Mr Treuhaft, I have just printed two souvenir editions of *Bunte Illustrierte* on the Queen and Prince Philip.

'I am going to send them to you and I would like you to go to Buckingham Palace and personally give them to the Queen.'

For a second I couldn't help laughing about the assignment, then I said it was very good idea, but it would be more impressive if I gave them to the German Ambassador. At his next audience with the Queen he could give her the publications as a present.

151

For a second the 'Senator' didn't reply, than he said, 'Treuhaft, that is a very good idea, you are a clever boy!'

So while I didn't get to meet the Queen, I did meet one of the most famous Royal dress designers of the 20th Century, Norman Hartnell. He also designed menswear and had clients including Noel Coward.

Norman dressed Elizabeth and Margaret as Princess brides-maids, but his most famous commission was the Coronation Dress for Queen Elizabeth II herself.

When Professor Heinz Scheibenpflug, Editor-in-Chief of the women's journal *Fuer Sie*, asked me to contact Norman about being on the Jury Board of the European Fashion competition in Munich, I wasn't surprised. Not only was he famous for his Royal creations, but he had also designed dresses for Vivienne Leigh, Marlene Dietrich and many big names of the period.

I had been the magazine's London correspondent for several years, but it was the first time I would have any connection with the Fashion world besides being just an attendee at a few fashion shows in London.

After several visits to his showroom at 10, Bruton Street, Norman agreed to represent the British section taking a part in fashion show.

Mr Hartnell and his press officer stayed at the Bayrischer Hof in Munich where the Editor of *Fuer Sie* had booked the room for the party.

A day after the competition I was asked to show our famous guest the city of Munich, as he was anxious to visit the Hofbrauhaus and enjoy a glass of real Bavarian beer.

First I took him to the Nympenburg Castle where the mad King Ludwig of Bavaria used to reside, and then to the Hofbrauhaus known not only for its famous beer, but also for where Hitler started an unsuccessful revolt on November 9, 1923.

Here, his press officer asked me if I could approach a

waitress and tell her what a famous guest she was serving and if she wanted an autograph from the dress designer of the Queen of England.

I went to the bar from which the waitress was serving and whispered that she had just served her glass of beer to the famous dress designer of the Queen of England, and that she should ask her guest for a special autograph to give the impression that she had recognised him.

A few seconds later the waitress approach Hartnell asking for his autograph, and as I was sitting next to him I could see how impressed he was, thinking that he was even recognised at the Hofbrauhaus in Munich.

A week after I returned to London I visited him again, this time not at his office in Bruton Street but at his private residence in Windsor. It was to give him a special issue of the publication *Fuer Sie*, which had published the story of his stay in the Bavarian Capital.

Hartnell invited me in for a cup of tea and I could see on the sideboard in his lounge all the signed photographs of the British Royalty for whom he had designed either their wedding dress or a special dress for the annual Ascot week in June.

When it was time to leave, Hartnell accompanied me to the car and shook my hand wishing me a pleasant return journey back to London.

Looking back at all the various assignments I have had as a journalist meeting the famous people I have either interviewed or having met on different occasion, Norman Hartnell was one of the most pleasant personalities I ever came across.

The next time I heard from publisher 'Senator' Franz Burda at *Bunte* was when he wanted me to find a master crime author. His name was Francis Durbridge and he had written two of the most successful TV series of the '60s, *Melissa* and *The Scarf*, which were not only a great success in England, but in Germany too.

In fact a German taxi driver told me once that the streets of Hamburg and Munich were empty when these shows played on TV, so that their work came to a standstill when the works of Durbridge were broadcast.

As a result of this, it came as no surprise that the new TV publication *Bild Und Funk* had been able to increase their circulation with a spread on Durbridge during a run of both series.

'Senator' Franz Burda was keen to show his admiration for the author and arranged a huge parcel of whisky and wine for him at Christmas. I was instructed to contact Francis Durbridge to give him the gift personally on his behalf.

However, to find him took some time. I knew that he didn't live in London, and soon found out that he was not very publicity minded either.

Luckily he had an agent Curtis Brown, who had an office near Covent Garden, so I was able to call by and explain why I wanted to meet the author of such crime masterpieces as *Paul Temple*, *The World Of Tim Frazer*, and the TV programmes I have already mentioned.

Maybe it was because I had such a generous gift, or that he thought that publicity in the German press would be good for Durbridge, that an interview was arranged at his press office.

On the day I went to meet him with a photographer I remember being very surprised. I was introduced to him at the reception desk and got into a tiny lift that took us up to a specially arranged interview room.

I found it difficult to believe that this small, rather ordinary looking man could be the genius writer I had come to meet. I suppose I was expecting a large, tough looking man who would not look out of place on the door of an East End nightspot, but instead Francis came across more like a civil servant.

Though he certainly wasn't pleased to be squeezed into

such a small lift, he didn't give me the impression that he had met or had anything to do with the many criminal types he had so successfully described in his books.

When it came to taking photos of him with the gifts from my publisher, he insisted that my photographer would only be allowed to take pictures if the labels on the bottles where not displayed.

'If I am seen with bottles of wine and whisky in the press, readers may think that I am an alcoholic. Also I have no intention of promoting alcohol,' he said.

'I appreciate the present from your publisher, but I will only accept the bottles if the present is not a promotion for either the magazine or the drink companies,' he told me very clearly.

I had to assure him that the gift was only in recognition of the success of his TV programmes in Germany, and that the picture was for the many readers who had written to the editor asking for a photo to be published of this famous author.

Eventually he smiled and the photos were taken, even though some were still taken with drinks on the table.

After this we spoke some more about his career, then he thanked me before leaving and returning to his country house outside London. As he left he said that he hoped that readers would soon have the opportunity to see his new TV plays *The Doll* and *The Game Of Murder.*

Recollecting my meeting with the famous author who died in 1998, I realise that Paul Temple was one of the most successful detective characters ever created for broadcasting.

Also in the late 1950s when representing the German weekly publication *Neue Welt Am Sonnabend* published in Düsseldorf, I heard from the Editor asking me whether I had good connections with editors in Fleet Street.

A personal friend of Emmy Goering – Mrs Paula Stuck von Reznicek – who had acquired the world rights of Emmy

Goering's memoirs had approached him. He was anxious to place the English speaking rights with a newspaper in England, and asked if I would be interested in translating them and offering the memoirs here on their behalf.

Mrs Stuck von Reznicek herself had some notoriety. She was a well-known tennis star in 1920s (who had played at Wimbledon) and once the wife of the famous German racing driver Hans von Stuck.

This approach from the Editor certainly surprised me, as he knew that I was Jewish and a survivor of two concentration camps, but I was still interested in offering the memoirs.

It was also an attractive offer as Mrs Stuck had obtained the authority to negotiate all rights

After I had received the German manuscript directly from Emmy Goering, along with confirmation that I should negotiate the English rights, I translated some chapters with a synopsis and offered them to the *Sunday Express*.

After receiving a negative response I went to the *News of the World* and later *The People*, but most Fleet Street editors were under the impression Mrs Goering was just trying to whitewash the crimes of the Third Reich committed by her husband. So on November 1, 1958, after much correspondence back and forth, I decided to visit Emmy Goering myself with my wife in Munich. We went to visit her in her flat near the famous Vier Jahreszeiten Hotel.

Mrs Goering was formerly known as Emmy Sonnenmann but had married the second most powerful man in the Third Reich. Hermann Goering was the man who once boasted that he would destroy London and lay two major cities of England to ashes, if it ever went to war with Nazi Germany. Yet even after the outbreak of the Second World War, the German Reich Marshall was so confident of victory that he declared, 'No enemy aircraft will ever penetrate German soil.'

Goering was not only one of the best showmen in the Nazi hierarchy, but one of the most important men around

Hitler, and a popular figure in Berlin as he was considered as a jolly fellow.

But was he less brutal than Himmler? Was he ignorant of the gas chambers of Auschwitz and Belsen? Did he prepare for war at the time when he was talking peace and gave great parties for the British Ambassador in Karin Hall, and arranged hunting excursions for Marshal Pilsudski and his Foreign Minister Colonel Beck two years before he pressed the button for the invasion of Poland.

When did the man next to Hitler realise that the war was lost? His suicide six hours before he was going to be led to the gallows aroused a sensation in the world press. Who gave Hermann Goering the suicide pill?

Emmy Goering was lying in bed when we arrived. She excused herself as she was just recovering from flu, but was prepared to see us because until now the leading editors in Fleet Street had rejected her memoirs.

When I introduced myself, I told her that I was a survivor of two concentration camps and that I was Jewish, to which she immediately said, 'Mr Treuhaft, I can assure you that I never knew anything about what happened in those camps. Hermann always told me that they were only for people to be re-educated should they offend the Führer and the Third Reich. He also told me that I should not interfere in politics.

'However once after I took the German Underground during the war to save petrol, the Führer called me personally to say that I should never use public transport again, as I was the wife of a Field Marshal. From then on wherever I went, a member of the Gestapo shadowed me and it was well known that Hermann never liked Himmler.

'Mr Treuhaft, you don't know how much I suffered during the last year of the war.' Now she told me how General Eisenhower betrayed her husband after the American General Stack and arrested Hermann a fortnight before the end of the war.

'Stack had an interpreter with him, but despite the fact that Hermann spoke perfect English, he still asked for an English translation of every word he spoke.

'Goering was assured by the American General over the telephone that he would have 'free passage' (not be arrested) and that they would meet the next day. Hermann had previously tried to contact Eisenhower and took his word of honour, but I remember that after seeing my husband enter a car and wave as he was driven off to prison it was the last I saw of him.'

I asked her whether her husband had ever considered coming to terms with the Allies, to which she replied, 'It was well known that my husband never wanted the war, and shortly after September 3, 1939 Hermann had approached some contacts in Sweden and suggested that Britain and Germany should work together.

'But as you know, Hitler refused to compromise and as late as 1943 Hermann mentioned to the Führer that we should find a way to negotiate a peace, but he wouldn't hear of it.

'A week before the end of the war, when Berlin was surrounded by the Red Army, Hitler learned that Hermann had tried to contact General Eisenhower and he dispatched an SS guard to our home with the order that Hermann should be shot for treason.

'But first Hitler sent the General Staff Chief of the Luftwaffe Koller saying that my husband shouldn't leave home as he was bringing an important message from Berlin.

'When Koller arrived he said that for the first time Adolf Hitler had admitted that the war was lost, and on being questioned on what the General should do he had replied, "Get in touch with the Reich Marshall who should negotiate with the enemy. He can do better than I."

'Koller had asked Hitler if he could say all this to the Reich Marshall, and Adolf Hitler agreed but he didn't give him any signed authority.

158

'My husband then sent someone to Dr Lammers, the leading lawyer of the Third Reich, who had stayed in Berchtesgaden. When he came up, Hermann asked him if the Führer's will was still the same, as my husband thought Hitler might have altered it because of the tension that had existed between them during the previous two years.

'Under no circumstances did my husband want to start negotiations without a written order from the Führer, so Hermann sent a cable to the Führer asking him to confirm the message from Koller.

'Hermann had wanted the authority to negotiate for peace two years before he told me, and asked Hitler several times for it. Now we were waiting hours at home for a reply when suddenly an armed SS man arrived with a signed document.

'But it was not the signed document he expected, Instead it said that Hitler himself was taking over complete leadership, and also accused Hermann of being a traitor and stripped him of all his titles.'

Well the rest is well known, but Emmy Goering told me once more that if Edward VIII had succeeded George V Britain would never have declared war on Germany.

Frau Goering didn't want to continue the conversation after this. On October 16, 1946, Hermann took a cyanide pill in prison, and when I asked Emmy how she thought he was able to receive it she wouldn't reply.

Most probably Hermann knew that the Nuremberg trial would find him guilty of war crimes and that he would been executed along with other Nazi leaders, but how was he able to find any poison in prison?

Sixty years later in 2005 a GI soldier declared that he had given Goering the poison but perhaps only the FBI and maybe this American guard know the actual truth about whether the pill had been smuggled in on the orders of President Eisenhower. He had broken his promise of a free passage, so maybe he was now saving Goering from the humiliation of going to the gallows.

After my meeting with Emmy Goering I approached several more newspapers with her memoirs, but it took another two years before an English edition was published in the USA and England.

After my return to London I received a letter from Emmy thanking me for my assistance in getting her memoirs looked at by leading newspapers in Fleet Street.

A few years later I saw the product of her husband's work when I went to Coventry. No less than 12,000 people were killed here during the war, and in 1962 I went to report on behalf of *Bunte*.

The German government had sent fourteen boys and two girls to help rebuild Coventry Cathedral which had been badly bomb damaged.

When I interviewed them they told of their surprise at how welcome they had been made to feel. Some of the locals even invited them round for dinner, although the foreman was strict about them not being out after 11.00 p.m., and that they must report for work each morning at 8.00 a.m. They were allowed just half an hour for lunch and they had to sleep in two Nissen huts (except the girls who stayed with local families).

The group did a lot for reconciliation between the people of England and German here in Coventry, but these missions weren't always as successful. During this period the German government sent other teams to help rebuild areas where the Nazis had caused distress, but their welcome had never been so generous as it was here in Coventry.

My report was recorded on a recent invention, the mobile tape-recorder. Such was the interest in this new invention that a picture of me using it while meeting the German group was used on the front cover of *Tape Recording Magazine*.

The next time I went to Munich, it was in 1965 with the

160

famous bandleader and conductor Mantovani. I had to accompany the guest of honour at the 'Bal Pare', an annual event held by 'Senator' Franz Burda. However in 1966 I stopped working for the Senator and took up a freelance position with a Malaysian newspaper.

This meant I could return to Munich again, but without the pressure of having to please a German Editor. It gave me an opportunity to properly analyse the former birthplace of the Nazi movement 20 years after the end of the war.

Chapter Thirteen

As I was paying my own expenses, it was out of the question to stay at my usual business hotel the Bayrischer Hof. Instead I stayed at the Bundesbahn, which was right inside Munich station, though prices at both had risen nearly 50 per cent since I had first stayed at them.

The strong D-Mark had once again given Germans great confidence and around Munich station there were foreign workers for whom Germany in the late '60s had become a paradise.

The German hotel staff in general were not as friendly as they used to be and I detected a self confidence that could almost be seen as arrogance, and I had seen this all before.

I met an old friend of mine, Alfred Jacob, who had been the Editor of the German film journal *Star Revue*. In the '50s I was his London correspondent, but we had lost touch until this trip to Munich.

Now he was President of a German-Arab Society and I went to visit him on the 14th floor of an impressive new building.

'Long time no see,' he said. 'I have put the champagne in the fridge for you. Gerd, welcome to Munich.'

After exchanging stories and memories of the past he said, 'The politicians don't know what they are doing in Bonn.

'First we weren't going to have nuclear weapons. Remember, they didn't trust us, we were all war criminals. Now they are talking about a neutron bomb on German soil.

'If you talk to the 20 and 30-year-olds they will tell you

163

to shut up because you were once a member of the Nazi party and responsible for the gas chambers of Auschwitz and Buchenwald. If you talk to the older generation they say you cannot go out after dark in the streets of Munich without getting mugged.

'That would never have happened under Hitler. Tell me, who is right and who is wrong?'

Alfred didn't wait for my answer. He continued, 'Both have a point, but the trouble is with the younger generation is that they don't want to work any more.

'Democracy, as you know it in England, has not found its roots in Germany yet. We have here a political vacuum between the past and the future, and the present leadership in Bonn doesn't know where it's going.'

I had no regrets about leaving Munich and was glad when a smiling Lufthansa stewardess showed me to a seat and it was time to fasten our seat belts.

I dozed off thinking about Munich, friends, and of my conversation with the late Count Montgelas (founder of the respectable Munich newspaper *Munchner Merkur*) shortly before the end of the Second World War. He had suggested when we met in London that if Bavaria got its independence back after the war, I should be its Youth Leader.

The weather was perfect on arrival back in London and I was glad to be home – despite the strength of the German mark and the falling value of the pound.

In the 1970s I began writing a column 'London Letter' with news from the capital and Britain in general submitted to newspapers around world.

With success in Malaysia, Ibiza, Jamaica, the Philippines, Nepal, Oman, Mexico and USA I continued to seek other markets and went to see my friend Michael at the Central Feature Agency on Fleet Street.

In the past I had helped Michael sell his own stories to the various German magazines I represented, and he was happy to help when I asked him if he had contacts with other foreign publications that were unrepresented in London.

'Well, you may just be in luck,' said Michael. 'I've just had a visit from an Arabian Prince who is looking for features for a new publication in Saudi Arabia *Arab News.* I'll give you his address.'

After returning home from Fleet Street I contacted the Prince and enclosed a copy of my London Diary.

At first I didn't hear anything, but I continued to send the column and after a third attempt I received a letter from the Editor-in-Chief. He was interested in my contribution, and offered me a monthly fee of £25.

Shortly after I heard from the Editor again, this time to inform me that I should contact the paper's London representative, a Mr Tony Purdy. So I arranged to meet Mr Purdy at the Scotch Corner pub in Haymarket, and my first impression was that he was not only a very likeable person, but he had very good knowledge of Fleet Street. (He had actually worked for the *Daily Express.*)

'We like your column,' he said after a short introduction. 'How much are they paying you already?'

'£25 a month,' I replied.

'Well, I would be happy to increase it to £60,' he said, to which I was a little surprised but happy to accept.

While we enjoyed another drink I mentioned to Tony that one of the big Fleet Street picture agencies was in financial trouble and might be taken over soon. He asked for some more information and I gave him the details.

Later, I found out that in less than a week Tony had not only managed to interest his Arab publisher in the picture agency, but they had bought it!

'I'll make you overseas manager,' said Tony when I met him again in Fleet Street, and he appointed me a special member of their new UK operation that they called the Saudi Research & Marketing Co.

Soon after, Tony was anxious that I should attend the Frankfurt Book Fair in order to make new contacts for their new agency. I agreed to go, but with such short notice I had to point out that I would have difficulties finding affordable accommodation. I needn't have worried as he agreed to cover all expenses including a stay at a very expensive hotel.

When I arrived at the book fair and paid my first visit to the Saudi Arabia stand, a member of the Egyptian Embassy from Bonn greeted me. 'I am so glad you are here,' he said with what sounded like a great deal of relief. 'I have to look after the Egyptian book stand, so you will have to represent the Saudi book stand until a representative from Jeddah arrives tomorrow.'

However, when the Jeddah rep arrived the next day, he couldn't speak either English or German so I ended up representing the Saudi stand for the remaining five days.

If this wasn't strange enough, when I returned to London my Tony Purdy had disappeared, and no one could tell me what had happened.

A successor, Chris Allsop had taken his place, and for the time being Chris wanted me to continue coming to the office twice a week to do a job. I was asked to contact foreign news agencies and newspapers to offer pictures from the agency, but after two months this came to a halt. Chris explained that he could no longer employ me as my fee was paid from the budget of the picture agency, and not from Jeddah direct.

So I contacted another newspaper in Kuwait, *Al Anba*, and was soon appointed their European correspondent with my own column that they translated into Arabic.

But it wasn't the last I heard from my former employers. Two months later I received a phone call from Chris Allsop inviting me for lunch at the Italian restaurant in Fetter Lane.

Saudi Research & Marketing wanted to start a new women's magazine, *Saidity*, and Chris asked me if I would like to join the company again as that budget for the new journal was covered by Jeddah.

I agreed an increased fee, and the new women's editor of *Saidity* was anxious to meet me, knowing that through my years in Fleet Street I had known all the different agencies and editors who might be interested to contribute to the new Arab women's journal.

It was now my job to negotiate with photographers, agencies for the Arab rights of their publication.

The editor of the magazine was very pleased with my service as she knew I had been the London correspondent of the German women's journal *Fuer Sie* and had good connections with German editors as well.

However when the Editor-in-Chief of *Saidity* left for Saudi Arabia and the publishing house moved from Gough Square to High Holborn, a new editor from Jeddah arrived and my service was no longer required.

Next I contacted the *Arab Times* in Kuwait, and to my surprise the new Editor-in-Chief was the previously vanished Tony Purdy, who not only remembered me, but also appointed me as his London correspondent with an office in Mayfair.

When I first arrived at the office in Park Lane I found more than 50 picture features on the floor, which where supplied by Camera Press, the well-known agency that syndicated picture features from Lord Snowdon.

It would have cost a fortune to send them all to Kuwait, so I phoned Mr Tom Blau, the Chief of Camera Press, and explained that I would only be sending a selection. Mr Blau replied, 'Mr Treuhaft, you are a very good journalist and I would like to work with you, but I must insist you send them all to Kuwait.'

I took his instruction and forwarded them all, but they all came back unused. This was typical of the waste of Arab money.

Tony Purdy's stay as Editor-in-Chief of *Arab Times* didn't

last long, and when he left my job there came to an end too.

After Tony disappeared from Kuwait he turned up a few weeks later in Cyprus and invited me to Nicosia. This time he wanted me to be London correspondent of a new Gulf TV Times, but the new publication never left the printing works.

I had a very enjoyable time in Cyprus before Tony left for Dubai and became adviser to a financial company. He promised to contact me again, but after having received two letters I didn't hear from him.

Four years later I learned that Tony had died of a heart attack in Cyprus.

My journalistic activity for Arab publications had come to an end and I returned to my weekly and monthly London Diary columns published in Sri Lanka, India, Nepal and Spain, although I did I join the *Oman Daily Observer* who published my column for more than three years.

Aside from my London Diary, I continued through the '80s and '90s representing foreign papers that had a particular interest in the British Royal Family.

However, whenever we dealt with the Buckingham Palace press office regarding foreign Royal visits, and also the UK visits of important foreign politicians, there were always very strict embargoes that had to be observed by both the British and foreign press.

It was understandable perhaps that some foreign publications wanted to be first with the news, but that could have serious consequences. A big lesson was learnt when Tom Blau, the boss of the Camera Press picture agency, once broke that embargo by supplying a certain picture ahead of time and he was fined £15,000 when a German customer printed it before the official date.

While still representing the German weekly *Neue Post*, I remember one special occasion when Prince Charles and Diana visited Rome.

I had a good friend in Fleet Street who had given me two royal transparencies taken just before the royal departure. There were strict instructions that they should not appear in print before the couple arrived in Rome.

But as I had them earlier than many of our rivals, I was able to send them to our Hamburg office where a special front cover of the magazine was prepared in advance.

As soon as the royal couple had landed in Rome we were on sale and this scoop really pleased the Editor-in-Chief.

Another scoop I was involved in concerned a picture of Prince Andrew returning from the Falklands war with his arms around two beautiful girls. It appeared in the *Daily Express* and I immediately contacted the paper and was able to agree a £5,000 fee for the German rights for the magazine *Quick*, with which I was also associated at the time.

I can look back on many events in the days when Fleet Street was an exciting and enjoyable place to work.

That was before many of the newspapers decided to move to other parts of London and Fleet Street became a ghost town as far as the press was concerned.

Chapter Fourteen

In 1995, 50 years after the end of the Second World War, the Jewish survivors from Berlin were invited back to the city they were forced to leave. Invitations were sent out all over the world to where they had been forced to try and make a new home. Now the Senate of Berlin had not only opened the gates of the former Reichshauptstadt to the Jewish survivors from Berlin, it had invited them back for a week at their expense.

More than 200 ex-Berliners from Brazil, North America, Australia and South Africa accepted, and from the United Kingdom I was one of three people who accepted an invitation.

The average age of the visiting group was between 70 and 75, and this was the first time I had visited Berlin since the wall had come down.

The half hour journey from Tegel airport to the Penta Hotel in the Nuernbergerstrasse gave the chance to speak to the taxi driver and I asked him how business was. 'It could be better,' he said, but was worried about the effects of the wall coming down.

'One of my colleagues who was driving through Eastern Berlin yesterday was murdered. They should never have dismantled the wall (referring to the Bonn Government). On the contrary, they should have made the wall higher. We are facing social unrest in West Berlin that has been exported from the East, and we have to pay higher taxes for people who don't want to work. Be glad that you are not living in Berlin.'

From the hotel I attended the reception given by Miss Katharina Ziebura on behalf of the Berlin Senate. We were given information on everyone else in attendance, and to my surprise I discovered that one of the guests had not only lived in the same street as I, but had been in the same two concentration camps, the same refugee camp, and in the same unit of the British Army. He lived only 30 minutes from my home in Hertfordshire.

The reunion of old friends and acquaintances was not the only purpose of the invitation. At a special reception, the Mayor of Berlin, Herr Eberhard Diepgen, wanted to assure his guests that the fear of the ex-Berliners of the resurrection of Nazism was unjustified. In fact the Berlin State would fight against any elements trying to undermine the democratic principles enjoyed by West Berlin since the end of the war.

He thanked us for accepting the invitation despite the bitter experiences we had all suffered under the Nazi regime.

However slogans like 'Auslander Raus' (foreigners out), 'Keine Juden Hier' (no Jews here), and the demolition of graves at Jewish cemeteries and at the former concentration camp of Sachsenhausen outside Berlin were in evidence. This brought fear to many of the guests who, accompanied by grandchildren, were visiting Berlin for the first time in 60 years.

I visited a friend who I had not seen for 53 years, and who lived on the Eastern side of Berlin. Her husband, who had died 12 years ago, was a fellow prisoner in a concentration camp.

As we wouldn't recognise each other, she asked me for passport identification before opening the door of her flat, and then excused herself saying, 'Gerd, we have to be so careful.'

She told me that since the wall came down, rape and murder had become daily atrocities and the rebirth of Nazism increasingly apparent. Unemployment was rising among the

172

young who only know the Third Reich from history books and are disappointed with democracy. Rumours were that the extreme right wing was getting financial support – and Berliners from both the West and East agreed that the demolition of the wall had caused unforeseen problems.

None of the political parties in Bonn at the time had a clear solution to dealing with the threat of a Fourth Reich, they were just keeping a close eye.

During my stay, several Berlin districts organised exhibitions and lectures about Jewish persecution under the Nazi regime from 1933 to 1945, so the Senate of Berlin at least should be given special credit for its efforts to oppose anti-Semitism. But I was happy to leave Berlin and share with the other guests the feeling that while there may be some forgiveness for what happened here, we shall never forget. And as for the future there are no guarantees.

In my life I survived a world war, the rise and fall of the Third Reich, can recall the Night of the Long Knives, Kristallnacht, and over a year spent in two concentration camps. This alone is an epoch of the 20th century for the history books.

Looking at the brighter side of these days, I attended major political events like the first United Nations gathering where I met Prime Minster Attlee, and interviewed stars of the film and theatre world – Elizabeth Taylor, Sophia Loren, Ingrid Bergman, Noel Coward, Walt Disney, Albert Lieven and Anton Wahlbrook.

As I left Berlin I remembered my school days and when one pupil sitting next to be scribbled a Swastika on one of my books. His father, Herr Kube, became Nazi Governor of East Prussia and was murdered before the end of the war. Another boy at school boasted that his father was Hans Otto Weber, a well-known undertaker who buried Friederich Ebert (the first President of the Weimar Republic and Germany's liberal Foreign Minister Gustav Stresemann). While on a school trip to Tempelhof Feld I saw Charles Lindbergh when he visited Berlin after his first crossing of the Atlantic.

I close my autobiography at the end of the 20th century, but looking to the future. The events of the first few years of the 21st century have inspired me to continue writing, which I do through my London Diary, published internationally through to this day.